Testimonials

"You've helped so much by doing v
fact that you can speak out about s
despite having Asperger's and there
my partner's world" so that I can make my family's life work
better.

Your voice is what helps him speak to me. He can't find the
words by himself but he can say "that's how I feel" or "I don't
worry about things like that." If nothing else, the curly hair
project has saved ONE family from destruction. Mine. That
sounds overly dramatic but it's not - it's totally true. And you
should be very proud of that."
Beth, UK

"What you're doing is amazing and you have helped me feel
a lot more open and honest about my odd ways. You have the
talent and determination to speak out for your fellow Aspies
and the way you are teaching NTs to understand AS, without
any lecturing, bias or glory seeking, is outstanding."
Becky, UK

"Bless you for the curly hair project. I live in the United States
in Michigan and have not found anything as helpful as your
Facebook page. My son has Asperger's and the explanations
are so clear. I'm going to recommend this to everyone I know."
Timberlea, USA

"I can't wait read the curly hair books. I'm hoping my son
Bailey will realise he's not alone when he reads them, as he
says nobody understands. Alis is the only person I have been
able to relate to and I always make sure I validate Bailey's
feelings now."
Katie, UK

"I just wanted to let you know that you inspire me and help me not feel as 'odd' and 'wrong' as I've thought myself to be; I'm not alone. You have also helped my partner understand certain aspects of the Aspie world and consequently he is able to grasp some of the things I have to deal with on a daily basis."
Lynsie, USA

"With gentle but effective understanding, Alis perfectly expresses interactions between Aspies and NTs. Clear and simple cartoons help to bring the message across in an easy to grasp way. Alis is very talented and has a gift for bridging the gap between people with Asperger's Syndrome and others who love them."
Linda, USA

"As an everyday person with no special knowledge of Asperger's whatsoever, Alis has helped me to understand the world from my friend's point of view much better. She writes in a clear and easy to understand style, with clear diagrams included where necessary. Altogether a very useful and enlightening read."
Clare, UK

"Sometimes your posts make me tear up - not in a bad way - it's just so great to see someone else "gets" it and knows exactly how I feel. Just when I think it can't be better you post something else."
Emily, USA

"My daughter is reading 'Asperger's and Me'. What makes this amazing is that she hates reading (has never read a book in her life) and struggles with comprehension. She understands everything you are saying. One page would normally have switched her off!"
Louise, UK

the girl with the curly hair

Asperger's and Me

Alis Rowe

Lonely Mind Books
London

The Girl with the Curly Hair - Asperger's and Me
978-0-9562693-2-4

Also by Alis Rowe

One Lonely Mind
978-0-9562693-0-0

The Girl with the Curly Hair presents The 1st Comic Book
978-0-9562693-1-7

The Girl with the Curly Hair presents The 2nd Comic Book
978-0-9562693-3-1

Have a look at Alis's Amazon Author page:
www.amazon.co.uk/Alis-Rowe/e/B00356H310

Websites:
www.alisrowe.co.uk
www.thegirlwiththecurlyhair.co.uk
www.womensweightlifting.co.uk

Social Media:
www.facebook.com/thegirlwiththecurlyhair
www.twitter.com/curlyhairedalis
www.twitter.com/alisthelioness
www.linkedin.com/in/alisrowe

ISBN 978-0-9562693-2-4

9 780956 269324

With special mentions to my family

and

Pierre, Beth, Euan, Heather and her children Eden and Alesh, Jannine, Kathryn, Kerrie and her nephew Nathan, Kirsteen, Kristina, Linda, Lisa and Stewart

Copyright

Printed and bound in the UK by Short Run Press Limited.

Short Run Press
Bittern Road
Sowton Industrial Estate
Exeter EX2 7LW

Preface

I am Alis, aka The Girl with the Curly Hair. I've been told that I am like no one you have met before. I am quirky, a bit eccentric, and definitely a lot of fun.

This book is about my experiences of growing up with Asperger's Syndrome, undiagnosed but always knowing I was different. I am now in my twenties and some scenarios from my childhood are just so crystal clear in my memories that it would be a shame not to write them down. I hope a lot of them will help others.

Even though the subject of mental health is quite a serious one, I have tried to make my book enjoyable and accessible to everyone, whether or not they have Asperger's Syndrome or are neurotypical. I have tried to include viewpoints from both sides with the aim that both "brain-types" can learn to understand each other better.

I think that although there is certainly some good information about Asperger's Syndrome available, a lot of it gives the wrong impression. It is not all 'doom and gloom,' and it is certainly not the "illness" that many people make it out to be. It is simply a different way of living. In fact, some people even glorify it to the extent that it has been made out to be "cool" and somewhat superior to the more neurotypical mind. I do not want to talk about Asperger's Syndrome being cool or superior. I do not believe that people with AS are "better" than their NT counterparts. I believe that we are all equal, the only difference is that people with Asperger's Syndrome are in the minority. This means there is work to be done in order to make information more accessible to the general public, which will raise awareness of our different minds.

Most "problems" in AS/NT relationships are caused by misunderstandings, miscommunication or those baffling Aspie meltdowns.

Imagine if an undiagnosed adult who had never heard about Asperger's Syndrome, suddenly came across a book, a poster or a magazine in a waiting room or while on the bus. They might read it and receive answers to questions that perhaps they had been asking their entire life.

Imagine how uplifting that would be?

Or what about the neurotypical person who stumbles across the same material, the husband or wife who spent years trying to make their marriage work but to no avail? The NT eventually gives up because, despite their hard work and emotion, the relationship seems doomed to fail. They might wonder what is wrong with them. Imagine them discovering Asperger's Syndrome and finally everything can be explained? This would be life-changing.

But we are all here living together on planet Earth, we need to learn to understand our differences, so that we can all be happy!

I love the diversity of human behaviour and culture. It is this diversity that makes the world go round.

Writing this book has been like taking a trip into the deepest parts of my mind. Life has been painfully hard for me but not in the conventional sense. Since writing this book, I have learned to love life. I have found closure in a world that has been extremely confusing for me.

I hope you enjoy my journey.

ALIS AKA THE GIRL WITH THE CURLY HAIR

Contents

Foreword

Hello! Welcome to my book; I'm really glad you found it. I am The Girl with the Curly Hair, aka Alis, and I am 24 years old. I live with my mum, dad and sister, in a town called Teddington in South West London. We have seven gorgeous cats (three Ragdolls, one Norwegian Forest, two Exotic Shorthairs and one British Shorthair), a hamster and love to dog-sit. Even though I have a lovely family and wonderful life at home, I've had issues with depression and extremes of mood most of my life. I can come out with lines like "I want to kill myself" or "I hate living" very quickly.

Ever since I was very little I've struggled with not knowing who I am and how I'm supposed to feel. I've always felt that I was in conflict with the world and I've always felt different inside; it's an innate, isolating feeling, but it's common for people to just tell me I'm extremely shy.

When I received a diagnosis of Asperger's Syndrome at the age of 23, it was a big relief for me. It made me understand so many things that had previously been really confusing. Finally, I feel able to explain why I think and act the way I do.

I've always found it to be extremely helpful reading about other people's experiences of Asperger's Syndrome. When I read, I can match up peculiarities in my personality with other women with Asperger's Syndrome. It is so uplifting. Their experiences make me feel less alone and less misunderstood. I wrote this book with the view that I could help someone else feel less alone too.

It's very common for people on the autistic spectrum to have additional difficulties. I have separate diagnoses of chronic depression, social phobia and suspected ADHD. For a lot of people on the autistic spectrum:

"Depression is the shadow side of Asperger's Syndrome and a sister to anxiety." (Rudy Simone[1]*, 2012)*

---

1 Simone, R (2012). 22 Things a Woman with Asperger's Syndrome Wants Her Partner to Know. London: Jessica Kingsley Publishers. 122.

I really like this quote; it explains so much.

I always knew something in my brain wasn't "wired" the same as most people's, but couldn't pinpoint it exactly. After bouts of anti-depressants, counselling for the depression and the uniqueness and misunderstanding that I felt, the confirmation of Asperger's Syndrome felt like an explanation for my life.

Since my diagnosis, I feel able to recognise how Asperger's Syndrome interacts with my life and, consequently I am a lot happier than I was before.

I suggest, that if you're not already diagnosed but you suspect you have this condition, you might find it helpful to consider getting a diagnosis too.

There is a great lack of awareness about what Asperger's Syndrome actually is. The general public have often heard about it, but may not really know what it is. This is not their fault because, why would a member of the general public be aware of Asperger's Syndrome unless someone they loved had the condition?

The hardest thing about having Asperger's Syndrome is that it is an invisible condition. Particularly in women, it may not ever be totally obvious. We may just be seen as quirky, shy, eccentric, difficult, or overemotional. Or outspoken and blunt! Before my family and I understood my Asperger's Syndrome, I think sometimes they felt I was being selfish, difficult, uncaring or intrusive. But inside I was a mass of feelings.

95% of the time I pass as "neurotypical" when I am relating to others. The other 5% is the display of my Aspie eccentricities, quirks, and stims. This is both a positive and a negative for me. It means I can live day-to-day without a stigma surrounding me, but unfortunately it also means that some people assume I'm either making it up, moaning, or exaggerating my difficulties.

In my own time, it is the other way round - I pass as 95% Aspie and only 5% neurotypical.

Tomorrow I will get up and leave the house, go into work and get on with things, my challenges totally oblivious to the people around me. The next day will be the same. And the day after.

I hope this book will improve the interface between people with Asperger's Syndrome and the rest of the world. Most people with Asperger's Syndrome are able and willing to work and live a "normal" life, with the right supports and adjustments. The main problem is that most people are just unaware of how they can help... but they can! So much!

So, let us begin our journey into the wearing but wonderful world that is

ASPERGER'S SYNDROME

or "AS." Sometimes the shortened version is easier to say!

I would like to say that I am not wholly comfortable using the word 'neurotypical.' I'm not convinced that such a huge, diverse group of people who do not have an autism spectrum disorder can be lumped together. For the purpose of this book however, I have used the description of neurotypical to mean anyone who is not on the autistic spectrum. I think we do need a way to refer to people who are on the spectrum and people who are not. Since this book is aimed at those with Asperger's Syndrome as well as their family and friends, the two groups are distinct groups that need to be differentiated from one another when we are discussing autism.

Before we begin...
A word about my use of language. This book is written in my own way. There has been some editing by a neurotypical (thanks Dad!) to make what I am trying to say understandable. But much of my own, quirky, a bit repetitive AS language remains. So, these are not careless grammatical errors or typos that you may spot, but my unique AS language. As such, I hope it helps illustrate and bring alive the AS world.

1.
My
Diagnosis

What is Asperger's Syndrome?

I never intended this book to be a book of facts, but rather a sort of story about my personal experience of having Asperger's Syndrome[2], so I won't go into too much detail here. There are lots of other books with information and facts about it. One of the most popular is The Complete Guide to Asperger's Syndrome by Tony Attwood[3].

So, that being said, **what is Asperger's Syndrome to me?**

Well, it's an enormous part of who I am. It presents many challenges, both good and not so good but I think that overall the good things outweigh the bad! You can't often see that I have AS, but you might notice there are certain things about me that are a bit different.

Every human being is different, and every person with AS is different too. I am good at writing, art, weightlifting and cycling. I have an excellent eye for detail and I'm very good at using computers. In certain things, I'm extremely quick thinking and reactive, and am able to find solutions to problems efficiently. In other things, I can be quite slow, particularly when trying to socialise or understand other people.

Even though I do like certain people and enjoy their company occasionally, I have problems socialising and get tired very easily. Most of the time, I am okay - and happiest - when I'm alone doing my own "Alis things."

Asperger's to me means having lots of quirks that let me experience life from a different angle.

What is AS to other people (neurotypicals)?

Having read over this book now that it's complete, I've discovered a lot of things not only about myself but also the world around me. This is in some ways more important because I have to adjust to living in a world that is predominantly non-autistic. I have to learn what works for me and what doesn't, so that I can be happy in this world! Otherwise, my life

---

2 DSM-5 has just replaced the name 'Asperger's Syndrome' with "autism spectrum disorder," but Asperger's is still a term many people know. I like it.

3 Attwood, T (2007). The Complete Guide to Asperger's Syndrome. London: Jessica Kingsley Publishers.

will just be 'one big slog.'

I realise just how hard it is for other people to really know what it's like to have Asperger's Syndrome. Even for my family who, have been there for me my entire life, who have come along to the medical appointments, who have helped me through all my meltdowns and shutdowns, and who have seen me go through depression and helped me come out the other side. In spite of being a part of all of these things, they still don't really know what it's like being me, having Asperger's Syndrome.

So, after having an epiphany, I've incorporated the grey boxes which I hope will help others see the world through my eyes. I want them to understand the actions and emotions of every little thing that someone with Asperger's Syndrome goes through every day. If I can't explain to others what it's like in my world, how can I expect them to support me? And I also need them to explain their world to me.

The Diagnosis

I was diagnosed with Asperger's Syndrome in 2012 at the Maudsley Hospital in London. It was a two hour journey on the train from my house in the rush hour. I was feeling very anxious, but also excited because I really desperately wanted to be diagnosed! My mum came with me. I needed her there for her love and support, and she was also required for the assessment.

My appointment was scheduled for 9.00am and I was glad that the people who came to meet me were on time. What happened next is really all just a big blur, but I remember being separated from my mum and we were both asked a series of questions by different people in different rooms. I spent about 4 hours with the psychiatrist, who asked me so many questions, it felt like he knew me inside-out by the time we'd finished!

The psychiatrist was a really nice man and he made me feel very at ease. I remember a few of the first things he said to me inside his office:

"I have coffee. Does the smell bother you? Would you rather I didn't drink it?"

"Are you okay to use this pen I've touched?"

It was very uplifting to be asked these questions. I wish everybody would always ask me these kinds of questions. I felt considered, accepted and cared for.

After a lunch break, my mum and I together were talked to by another member of the team. He provided the final diagnoses of Asperger's Syndrome, social phobia and depression. An enormous weight had been lifted and I felt hugely relieved - almost "high."

I am a chemist so it seemed quirky for me to put in this illustration. If you don't know what it means, see footnote[4] below!

Before we left the hospital, the psychiatrist needed to photocopy some papers for us to take home. I asked him how long it would take to photocopy them.

"Approximately ten minutes," he replied. "I don't want to say ten minutes in case I'm a little over and upset you!"

My mum and I both smiled. Fourteen minutes later he came back with the papers and then Mum and I went home.

What a wonderful day it had been!

---

4 NHS. (2012). SSRIs (selective serotonin reuptake inhibitors) . Available: http://www.nhs.uk/conditions/
SSRIs-(selective-serotonin-reuptake-inhibitors)/Pages/Introduction.aspx. Last accessed 5th Nov
2013.

2.
My Life at School

"An overwhelming desire to be away from my peers..."

I wasn't really sure how to begin - or even structure - this book. The thing about my Asperger's Syndrome is that it can't really be broken down into different sections. AS is my identity and way of living. I can't just split it up into sections because all the sections would end up overlapping. I think my Asperger's Syndrome looks a bit like this:

This is my "wrong planet." It is a tangled web of all the things that make up my Asperger's Syndrome, including anxiety, depression, OCD, ADHD, hypersensitivity, emotional sensitivity, giftedness, individuality, etc.

I'm going to start by writing about some experiences at school, because they're probably some of my earliest, most tangible memories of really standing out amongst everybody else.

Nursery and infant school were not too bad, although my mum says I used to run out of school because I did not want to stay. Teachers always tried to get me to play in groups of girls instead of with my best male friend.

At primary school, the teachers used to say to me, "Why don't you go and play with the girls, Alis?" But I always only wanted to play with my best friend, who was a boy. He and I were inseparable for many years and are still in touch now.

> I think that if you have AS and get on well with one particular person, you should be encouraged to be with them. Friendships are important because we find them so hard.

I'll always remember this one time, I asked the teacher for a 'Desk Move' because I wanted to sit somewhere different. We had the Desk Move (where you get to move your place in class so you can choose who you want to sit next to), and I ended up on a table with five of the naughtiest boys in the class! The teacher said to me, "Alis, don't you dare ask me if you can move ever again". I guess she was disappointed with where I'd ended up sitting?

I really hated secondary school. I was bullied for being so quiet. What a strange reason? I'm still traumatised by the mockery of my peers and even some of the teachers. Some of the things I remember people saying are:

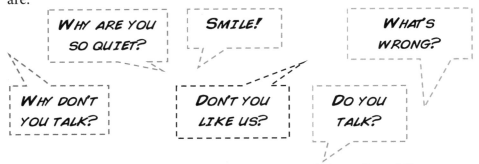

WHY ARE YOU SO QUIET?

SMILE!

WHAT'S WRONG?

WHY DON'T YOU TALK?

DON'T YOU LIKE US?

DO YOU TALK?

Some of the children used to jump out at me and shout "speak!" as though I was their pet dog.

YOU NEED TO TALK MORE

YOU'RE VERY SHY

I suppose it was the combination of being quiet and socially awkward that made me an easy target for bullying. Honestly, I really did just have nothing to say most of the time. Small talk had never come naturally and I struggled to follow the conversations that happened at the same time. I wasn't interested in the same stuff as other teenage girls. As well as this, I always felt I had this kind of "barrier" all around me, which made me physically unable to speak at times. Now I know the barrier was Asperger's Syndrome.

The more people made comments about my quietness, the more conscious of it I was and the lower my self-esteem became. It was a cycle.

I should have told my parents or teachers. If you have a child with AS, make sure they know what bullying is and that it's OK to 'tell' on bullies.

There were two girls I spent time with at secondary school. Although they were really nice, I never truly felt "connected" to them, but I'm not sure why. The other children seemed to make friends so easily. The two girls and I each had our own quirks and were made fun of for different reasons. But we did stick together and it meant I always had a partner for P.E.

Throughout the whole 5 years of secondary school, I just remember having this endless, **overwhelming** desire to get away from my peers. Most of my school days were spent watching the clock and I'd get really fidgety and agitated at 3.15pm (which was home time). I felt anxious and panicky whenever teachers were late in letting us leave. As soon as the class was dismissed, I was always the first one to leave - very, very quickly. I actually remember one of my classmates asking me why I was walking so quickly on my way home.

Even though I enjoyed a lot of things like art, computers and tennis, I avoided all extra-curricular activities. I just always wanted to be alone and away from everyone at school. Often my two girl friends would ask me over to one of their houses in the evenings or at the weekends, but I always said no and I dreaded being asked. They regularly rang my phone but I always avoided picking up or phoning them back. It was never my intention to appear rude and ungrateful; after all, they were just school friends being nice. I did appreciate them thinking of, and including me, but it was weird because I had simultaneous feelings of both wanting them to include me and not wanting them to include me. I often felt left out when the two of them met up outside of school without me but I had no idea what these feelings meant; I was so confused. I just didn't seem to be as "sociable" as all the other kids, who seemed to have endless social energy and enjoyed lots of interaction with others.

My experience of school was extremely stressful and overwhelming (I use this word a lot, but it's just perfect at describing a lot of my feelings). The sheer stress of having to be around people for a regimented six-hours-a-day-five-days-a-week, was just too much.

Like many with Asperger's Syndrome, I have sensory challenges. At school there was so much noise - kids laughing, teachers shouting, school bells and fire alarms; and so many people - the corridors were so overcrowded you could hardly walk through them without bumping into someone. There were so many faces, all different ages and backgrounds, some of them really quite frightening in both looks and behaviour. I remember when a boy threw a chair across the classroom, it really scared me but the teacher didn't do anything about it. The kids also used to push and shove one another in the corridors, just for fun. It was ridiculous. I felt so out of place, unsafe and incredibly distressed.

I always wanted to be at home and carry out my usual "Alis things." I needed to be in my house in my own space and comfort. I so badly needed those quiet evenings and weekends when I could be alone to rest up and recover from the frenzy of the past week. The way I describe the need for those "alone times" now, is that they are my "rebuilding times." The stresses and strains of everyday life break bits of pieces from me and I have to reconstruct myself every day.

I think it's important for parents and teachers to realise that it's totally OK if your child appears most happy on his or her own.

As a child and well into my teens, my granny would come and collect me after school every day. Even when I was 16 she'd be come and pick me up. I loved the care and the safety she provided and she was my best friend throughout school (and she still is). Granny and I would be at home together and do cooking, drawing and painting, or we'd play Monopoly. I really enjoyed doing these things at home.

I was always what you would describe as "shy," but I was actually very aware of this from a young age and actively wanted to not be like this. When I was about 12 I begged my parents to send me to Drama School (classes for acting, singing and performing etc. that ran at the weekends), because I thought that it would magically "convert" me from shy to confident in the space of a few weeks. I had a lot of exciting visions about how the new, improved, confident me would be! What happened was, I ended up attending just one class and I hated it so much that I never went again. My parents were a bit mad because it was a really expensive course and the school wouldn't refund their money.

Don't ever push your child to be more sociable. Aspies need less time socialising and more time being alone in order to manage.

I don't remember exactly what happened that made me hate the class so much. I know I was very shy and very quiet and immediately aware I didn't fit in. Everyone else already knew one another, they all talked and laughed and included each other in their groups. I was generally ignored by everyone, even the teachers. I guess it was the Asperger's barrier, showing its face again. In that moment, I just wanted to be 'normal.' I wanted to break the glass wall around me and experience life in the same way that the other children did. I felt very different - a "freak," a social pariah.

It is not always the diagnosis or "label" that makes a child a target for bullying. It's just obvious when a child does not quite fit in, just from the way he or she 'hold' themselves.

After that, I hated more than ever, anything that involved other children. I started to feel very, very lonely, sad, strange and different. I just kept wondering, "why am I like this?" Just why did I find it so unbearably hard to make friends? As a teenager, I experienced this "inability" to actually be like everyone else. The teenage years are fragile, traumatising times for anyone who's a bit different.

Friendship and its expectations of reciprocity can be exhausting for teenagers with Asperger's Syndrome, even though we often really want friends. The expectations of friendship, such as the phone calls, the girl talks, listening to other people's feelings... can be overwhelming.

When I left school to go to college to study A levels, I tried hard to be more outgoing because I thought it could be a new start where nobody knew me and had no history to judge me on. Happily, I made a couple of friends and successfully studied my subjects at college. By the time I left, although my confidence had improved greatly, unfortunately the real internal damage had already been done. When I was about 17 I started to understand that I really was quite different from other people my age. Even though I had some friends at college, I didn't actively pursue the relationships outside of the college environment; to me they were always just classmates who liked the same subjects.

For many years my social outlet was a simulation video game, where I could create characters and make their worlds. My emotional outlet was my creativity, through writing, drawing or painting. Throughout my adolescence, I never stopped writing. It was a way of expressing the misery and isolation I felt.

And so it was... by 17, I knew for certain that I was clinically depressed, extremely anxious and very lonely.

How my late diagnosis came to be...

Females in particular, are often diagnosed with Asperger's Syndrome when they are much older than their male counterparts. There is a tendency for females to be more disguised and we often have the ability to "blend" into situations. Unfortunately, due to this, many females with Asperger's Syndrome are left without a diagnosis or, as in my case, are diagnosed as an adult. Some girls don't even show autistic symptoms until puberty. I imagine it might be like women who realise they are gay in middle age, even though they've had boyfriends or even been married.

'Girls are more likely to suffer in silence.' (Tony Attwood[5], n.d.)

I agree. Personally, I am aware that very early on I picked up social cues and had the ability to adapt myself in order to "fit in." People often described me as just being very quiet or overly sensitive. I now realise that these personality quirks and

challenges were actually Asperger's Syndrome 'meltdowns', and not just

---

5   Attwood, T. (n.d.). Girls and women who have Asperger's syndrome. Available: http://www. tonyattwood.com.au/index.php/about-aspergers/girls-and-women-who-have-aspergers. Last accessed 16th Sep 2013.

"that time of the month" or depression. Something else *had* indeed been going on too.

 Now I understand just why I needed so much time on my own and why school was so unbearably stressful for me. In essence, my entire childhood was spent wearing a sort of "mask" for the world; a mask that I could only take off when I got home. This mask-like quality of acting as normal as  possible was, however, extremely tiring! Endlessly trying to fit in 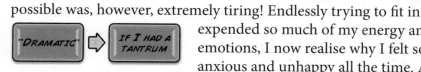 expended so much of my energy and emotions, I now realise why I felt so anxious and unhappy all the time. All my suffering was internalised and consequently I always appeared passive and shy. This quote really resonates with me:

'AS boys often appear like "little professors," who are experts in one subject, but AS girls are more like "little philosophers."' (Susan Moffitt[6], 2011)

I was always known in my family to be too deep a thinker and I remember my dad was always telling me I thought too much. Between the ages of 14 and 16 I was obsessed with God and the meaning of life; I read the Bible and the Koran; I just wanted to understand the things that science couldn't teach me. I remember in school or whenever I was outside of my house, the most important thing to me was to get home so I could philosophise about my life. I was always thinking, always analysing. No wonder I was exhausted.

If your child is showing similar symptoms, keep an eye on them. I would have found it invaluably helpful to have known about AS when growing up. Leave a book lying around, a webpage open, pin a leaflet on the calendar... a little exposure to AS is a good place to start. Just let them know that AS exists, same as Down's Syndrome, depression, broken bones, etc.

---

6   Moffitt, S. (2011). Asperger Syndrome in Girls More Common than Once Thought. Available: http://www.autismkey.com/asperger-syndrome-in-girls-more-common-than-once-thought/. Last accessed 2nd September 2013.

Being a 'Tomboy'

When I was little I was always described as a 'Tomboy'. From as young as a baby, all my friends were male. My parents have photos of me from my childhood where I was the only girl but surrounded by all these boys. At some of the parties I went to as a child, I was the only girl.

I can't say I really remember why I was like this, I just naturally seemed to befriend boys. I used to try and act like a boy and often wore boys' clothing. I loved playing sport and enjoyed toy cars, dinosaurs and computers. For several years I only wore football T-shirts and branded trainers, when all the other girls were wearing pink, frilly things and wearing their hair in ponytails.

Gender confusion

All the confusion I felt about my gender didn't really hurt me until I was about 11. Before then, I was just a happy, rather eccentric, hyperactive child who loved kicking footballs around. I just pleasantly existed, had no worries and felt pretty awesome and free. To be honest, as a young child I don't think the cultural expectations regarding gender ever clicked, I was always just "me." If anyone made fun of me for wearing "boy trainers", I was bemused. I knew that men and women had biological differences but, looking back it never seemed to register with me that we were supposed to act differently too.

The older I got, the more aware I was I might've been born the wrong sex. TV programmes, magazines, films and books taught me about gender differences, but still I could not relate to women. I was, in personality and spirit, a teenage boy. I never felt connected to other girls.

Growing up, my very favourite thing to do was to write stories, but my stories were always dreamed up and written where I or the main character was male. Writing as a male was just so natural and so easy. My interests were always more male- than female-orientated, I just naturally gravitated towards "male" clothing and hobbies. At 24, two of my favourite hobbies are computers and weightlifting. I don't like shopping for clothes and have no interest in makeup or fashion. I don't like women's magazines, weddings, and have no interest or desire for marriage or children. It's really odd how society has built up these stereotypes...

At school, I just kind of "existed." It was as if I just floated around, trying not to be noticed. Although, of course, I was noticed, being socially awkward and so quiet I couldn't help but stand out! Nevertheless, at school my whole personality was concealed; I felt like no one and nothing. I wasn't a person nor a particular gender. It was only at home I could relax and finally be "myself," whoever that was...

I had nothing in common with other girls. When they were interested in boys and fashion, I was interested in simulation video games, building websites, and writing stories. It was really hard trying to fit in; I practised and "learned" to know the latest fashion trends and pretended to think Leonardo Di Caprio was hot, just because everyone else thought so too. But at home I was myself, shut away in my own world, doing my own Alis things.

I was "the philosophiser" at home and spent hours pondering over my gender and sexuality. All through my teenage years, I was so muddled up. I was confused whether I was a lesbian or a boy in a girl's body. I used the internet to read up about these things (I was very good at research and using the computer) and I felt a little better when I realised it wasn't that uncommon for young people to have these sorts of questions and feelings. I felt comforted, but still very jumbled up inside my head. I guess having Asperger's Syndrome amplified my confusion. Learning about Asperger's Syndrome as an adult, I notice that gender problems are quite common among us.

For a while, when I was about 18, I made a conscious effort to join in and do some of the feminine things I was supposed to do. There were just a couple of years when I conformed to the female gender roles because I desperately wanted to fit in, particularly at my new college where no one knew me. I didn't want to be bullied or be that lone girl again. I didn't want to repeat how it had been at school. I did wear makeup for a time and made a big effort to chat and connect with some other girls, but deep inside I still felt very lost and lonely. It was all a tremendous act. Finally, at 24, for most of the time I am comfortable being Alis without acting.

> It was hard at the time but now I'm an adult I can look back and say with reservation that I am glad I had some difficulties with NTs during my school days. It's made me understand other people better. But would I conform if I had those teenage years again? Maybe not.

It's taken many years but finally I can say that I'm "content" being female, even though I don't particularly "feel" feminine. If I had to describe my gender I'd describe it as androgynous. I seem to have a blind-spot to gender in society. I can distinguish between males and females in real life but, for me, I seem to be a sort of blend between the two but not fitting into either one. I am a "nothing" inside a woman's body. As for "fancying" guys and my own sexuality, well that's all very befuddled too.

> Now I think it's always best to just be yourself. People who find you will like you for you. I understand that fitting in is important when you are young but remember, you'll probably never see those people again after school. Be proud to be different!

3.
The Normal Mask

What exactly is the "normal mask?"

It's quite a common thing amongst those of us with Asperger's Syndrome, to put on a "normal mask" whenever we have to face  the world. Girls especially, tend to be highly capable of appearing "normal" and that's why we're so often undiagnosed. The normal mask represents an "autistic person in hiding."

Over time and through different experiences, **I have learned how to be social**. I have 'high-functioning Asperger's Syndrome,' which to me means I am more able to compensate for my communication and social difficulties through logic and reasoning. As someone with Asperger's Syndrome, I am fortunate to be fairly adept at communicating and being social. I don't think you would initially think I was on the autistic spectrum if you talked to me for the first, second or third time. It's sad that for many females, we've perfected our masks so well, that by the time we're eventually diagnosed, a lot of people don't even believe us (more about this at the end of the book).

When I think about my bouts of depression I notice that they are almost always triggered by some kind of social interaction. My depression is probably brought on by my endless acts of conforming - just trying to be normal and act "normally" around others My normal mask looks a bit like this overleaf:

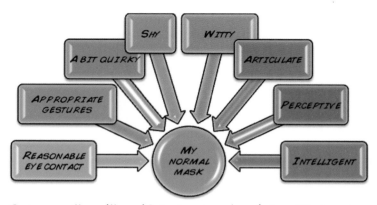

But my "real" self is trying hard to fit in· I am remembering to make eye contact, even though it feels more natural not to· I have an ongoing narrative inside my head, making sure I say the right thing and nod at the right time· I ensure I do small talk· Sometimes words just "come out of me," as though they have been rehearsed millions of times· I do not therefore, always say what I mean· Sometimes I would like to·

The thing is, most of these things haven't come instinctively to me. I have learned to be this way over many years. So, although in public I may come across as sensitive, kind, bright, a bit quirky and overall rather lovely (so people tell me!), it takes an enormous amount of effort to be this way all the time. People like me on first meeting; I'm told I give a good first impression and I can do "everyday conversation."

My avoidance of people and social situations is not meant to come across as a total negative. There are lots of people I do genuinely like! I just get very tired, very easily.

But after even small amounts of social activity, I continually find myself feeling exhausted from the effort and have to retreat to my home to do my solitary Alis things - writing, weightlifting, reading, computers.

As a parent, don't nag your child to be "like the other kids." It will make them feel extremely upset. Accept them for who they really are! "Neurotypical" is not equal to "good."

I have to socialise every day, to varying degrees. It doesn't matter how much or how little socialising I do - before, after and preferably in between I have to have breaks to rebuild. I get fatigued having to wear the normal mask. As soon as I step outside of my house, the mask goes on and with it comes a continual anxiety that's like a little worried dog sitting on my shoulder.

I love my family because they see, live with and wholly accept the special person beneath my mask. They understand my need to retreat or close off from the world; it's just never questioned. I don't have to ever explain myself, it's very uplifting. Unfortunately though, my family also get to see the worn out, anxious, depressed, unhappy side of me. It's only at home I can be this way, due to the disguise of the normal mask. I wonder if relationships with the closest people are in some ways the hardest ones? I've always been most happy being at home - I feel safe and almost touch a beautiful state of "enlightenment."

It gets better as you get older. I am now a lot more self-aware and know my limits. I accept that I can have fun socialising, I just need more time to rest up afterwards.

Although I am an introvert and my hobbies are solitary, I love being with my family who accept me for who I am. They don't push me into talking or attending social events because they know my personality, my limits and my boundaries. Staying close to my family - who know everything about me, my idiosyncrasies, quirks and love me unconditionally - combined with staying away from other people, makes me happiest day to day because I feel that I function at a depth that most people do not. I love being with my family but, at the same time, I love being alone. I really enjoy it when everyone is at home, but we're all doing our own individual things. My dad and I share our computer space. We sit on the same desk but at opposite ends. I can sense he is there but it's totally okay not to interact all the time.

At the (wise!) age of 24, I contemplate whether it's better to just unleash my Asperger's flat out, rather than expend so much energy being someone I'm not. I don't know if I'll ever truly have the confidence to be completely "free" of my normal mask, but the older I am the more comfortable I feel in just being myself and not having to conform.

Building the mask

My childhood is a bit of a blur to me, so I often wonder exactly how I constructed my normal mask. I feel really lucky to have had a neurotypical sibling; I think having my sister was a big help in having to grow up with AS. I was always comfortable with her, she was part of my "routine." Even though we fought sometimes, we used to play together in the paddling pool or on the climbing frame, and we'd ride our bikes and look after our pets together. I can imagine that if I'd been an 'only child', I would've grown up with fewer social skills.

Despite being introverted, I've always been really interested in other people and how they interact with the world around them. A deep thinker and keen to learn whatever I can, I'm always watching and listening to other people and I really like watching soaps and TV series. I often feel as if I'm on the outside looking in.

> Keep an eye on your daughter with AS. Sometimes it might look as though she's in another world. We tend to live in our imagination and can escape into fiction, animals or nature.

When I was younger I'd have conversations in my head. I created two or more characters and I would have them talk to each other. I'd entertain myself for hours doing this. It felt so easy to make up stories and conversations. I've written stories ever since I learned to write. I am very easily able to replicate the way real life people talk in my narration. I also understand and convey my characters' emotions well. But in the real world - it's not so easy.

It is sometimes said that people on the autistic spectrum lack imagination, but this definitely doesn't apply to me. I have a very vivid imagination and I really enjoyed playing imaginative games with my sister as a child. We had toy building bricks, Barbie dolls, Swiss animal families and toy animals. I have very clear memories of this and I remember being really disappointed when she grew out of the playing that I still craved for. I matured a lot later than my sister, despite being older. I enjoyed arranging our plastic toy animals in orderly lines; and while she was making up stories with dolls, I was enjoying writing out school timetables!

So I've never had trouble creating imaginary scenarios in my head - in fact, I suppose I did spend most of my childhood pretty much "existing" as someone else. I love, love, love telling stories. I loved computer simulation games where I could construct things like towns, roads and houses; it was really cool being able to create my own world. My favourite memories of childhood are the ones in which I'm writing or drawing - both hobbies that I've carried on to now. I write novels, draw and paint, and even sell some of my crafty things.

I wonder whether my imagination and ability to write so smoothly comes from all my people-watching. The main reason I like watching soaps and series on T.V. is because you get to follow the characters over a long period of time and observe them interacting in lots of different situations. I like seeing how characters develop. In my own stories, my strongly creative side is able to give a character so much depth. When I'm heavily engrossed in writing a story, I even fantasise about my characters because I'm just so immersed in them, even if they are not real.

I live inside my own mind. I prefer to be in it rather than out of it. Sometimes I feel sad because the world that is in my head does not truly exist. There is only the world outside. I don't get bored and I'm never really searching for things to do. My mind is my favourite toy.

People with Asperger's Syndrome are often pretty good at keeping themselves occupied.

4.
My
Conformation
Years

I did not really want to say much about what I call my "conformation years." However, for the purpose of this book I have put my reluctance aside because I think this chapter will be extremely helpful to others.

What were the conformation years?

I was very unhappy during my time at secondary school (age 11-16). I went from having a small number of friends at primary school to being a very quiet, very withdrawn child. When I was younger, the other children were attracted to my energy and my quirkiness. At secondary school however, being a bit different was no longer seen as "cool." It was much cooler to fit in and all be the same. Consequently, I became an outsider and I was a victim of bullying.

I spent my time with two friends, who were also misfits in their own way. The reason I ended up as part of their group was actually because we'd all been at the same primary school. Even though we were in different classes, I recognised them and they were familiar faces on a very scary first day at secondary school. Everyone had to gather around in the big school assembly hall and wait to be assigned to their new form groups.

I spent all my time at school with these girls, who were my 'friends' at the time. I was never able to make 'friends' with anyone new. I felt it was expected that children who were my age had friends and did things together, although I didn't actually have a desire to make friends with anyone - I was always happiest being on my own. But going around school on your own wasn't seen as normal and it made you stand out. In hindsight, the biggest reason why I probably stayed with these two girls was as a means of protection - if I was a loner there'd be yet another reason for people to pick on me.

It was good that I had two friends that I could partner up with for P.E. and group work, which I always dreaded, but had to do. Whenever possible I tried to pair up with one of them. If I had to work with anyone else, it was horrendous. I was so shy and anxious around other kids - and sometimes I was mute. I absolutely hated it when the teacher made me work with someone different. Their reason being, "it's good to learn to work with different types of people" and "it's good to be out of your comfort zone sometimes." The teachers did not realise that that's exactly what I could not deal with. Every night I had shutdowns and I just wanted to be alone.

As all of us grew into teenagers, things got more and more difficult for me. It seemed like everyone around me was into wild alcohol abuse, cannabis, late night partying, and underage sex. I could not relate to this teenage fixation on dating and having an attraction to the opposite sex. One of the most upsetting and hardest things I had to deal with was when my two friends began to change into young women, just like the rest of my peers. Suddenly they were no longer interested in video games and school work, preferring to talk about boys and fashion instead. Whereas all the other girls talked about the boys they thought were cute or who had a crush on who, I did not share their interest. These girls were experiencing romantic and emotional feelings that I just did not experience. I was so aware of this difference and I felt so, so lost. I was losing the only two people at school I had the confidence to connect with. I was never very close to them initially, but now it felt as though I was even further away.

Asperger's Syndrome is like living inside a glass jar when the rest of the world is on the outside. I can see all the people and things around me but I can't quite touch them. I call this 'Glass Jar Theory.'[7]

The older I got, the more I learned to fit in. I learned to wear makeup and read celebrity gossip magazines. I watched soaps and took an interest in the films that were showing at the cinema. I did not want to stand out any more than I already did. I did all of these things because I had nobody else at school but these girls, and I could not lose them. If I lost them, P.E., drama and other group activities would be even more painful and soul-destroying. That's how I felt. For the whole of school, it was like my soul was being broken apart, every single day.

---

7 Rowe, A. (2013). The Asperger's Syndrome 'Glass Jar Theory'. Available: http://thegirlwiththecurlyhair. co.uk/girl-curly-hairs-guide-aspergers-syndrome-socialising/. Last accessed 7th December 2013.

At home, I could disentangle myself from the web I was caught up in at school. At home it was acceptable to ignore teen fads and clothing styles. Evenings, weekends and holidays were spent inside the house, all day, every day, playing video games or using the computer. I was most happy doing these things, on my own. Home was my safe haven from rejection, isolation and bullying in the cruel world of secondary school. I could wear the same comfy clothes day in and day out.

Weekends and school holidays were my milestones. I had a big calendar and ticked off the term days with gold stars. "If I can just last three more weeks... two more weeks... one more week, it'll be okay. Then I will be on holiday for a long time." The last day of term was always a huge relief. The holidays were wonderful, but they were spoiled by endless nightmares of how little time I had left before school began again. Every day was a day closer to school and a day closer to depression. As the end of the summer holiday approached, I'd remind myself that I still had my birthday and our bank holiday weekend left - this meant there were still two significantly good events to come before term started, which made time slow down.

The only thing that kept me going was when I reminded myself that every day closer to the new school term was also a day closer to completely leaving school forever. It was only this vision that kept me going. I don't know how I survived, but I did it... I could never, ever do it again.

I understand that the teenage years are often the hardest ones - whether you are NT or AS. I don't think mainstream schools are suitable for children with AS. The pressure to conform is tremendous, it's usual for teenagers to face constant bullying and rejection. As parents, if the pressure on your child to conform is too much for them and the teaching staff are uncooperative, decide whether it's in your child's best interest to find another school or enter specialist education.

I feel that emotionally I matured three years later than my peers. When I was 17, I could finally comprehend what others had been going through at 14. For a time my priorities changed - I was more interested in making new friends at college. I could recognise why teenagers wanted to have boyfriends and girlfriends.

College was different from school, because it was much more flexible and I was studying only my favourite subjects (Biology, Chemistry, Computing, Physics and Maths). I chose to go to a college where very few people from my secondary school were going. I wanted it to be a fresh start, a place where no one knew how "uncool" I was. Having observed and been close to neurotypical girls at school meant I knew exactly how I needed to behave in order to fit in and make friends. At this age, I was extremely aware of my peers and, to an extent, I wanted what everyone else wanted. That included boyfriends.

Boyfriends

Despite the fact I never had any sexual feelings towards boys, I remember feeling sort of under pressure by society to start dating. I enjoyed the company of some boys and I liked the look of some of them too - but those "electric," "kinky" feelings that I heard other people talk about, I never experienced them.

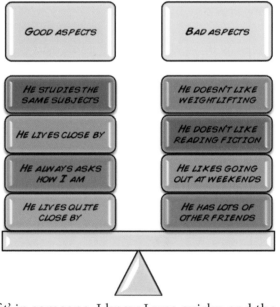

By the time I was 23, I'd been in three proper relationships. None of my partners were met at school, college or university. On the contrary, I met them on the internet. I never seemed to have any luck dating people I came across in real life, and I was never sure why. I was just unable to connect with anyone. I enjoyed some aspects of the personalities of some of my male friends, but then there were many more aspects I did not like. I could never find the 'perfect fit' in someone. I knew I was quirky, and the everyday people I knew, were not. I could weigh out the good and bad aspects of boys easily.

On the internet, it was a lot easier to suss a person out. Over several years, I'd been on quite a lot of dates. I gained a lot of life experience during this time. I remember feeling as though I wanted a boyfriend, but I wasn't exactly sure why, because my favourite past time was so obviously spending time on my own. Looking back, I think that I was conforming to what I thought our society expected of young women my age. These dates and boyfriends did not make me happy, but they gave me a lot of insight into the neurotypical mind. I am appreciative of this, because I think I am better at coping in everyday social situations. My uncle used to ask me, "why do you want a boyfriend?" and I used to tell him, "Well, it's what you do isn't it? I'm supposed to be married before I'm 30." At the time, I honestly thought this is what I was supposed to be doing...

At 17 or 18, my normal mask was near flawless. I'd get up one hour earlier than necessary, so I could do my hair and makeup before college. I went out with my friends for the first time in years, had some late nights, and relished in the attention I received from boys. It was a phenomenon for me how, when I put some makeup on, wore a skirt, had a big smile on my face, and spent time in shopping centres or cinemas, people were so much more open in wanting to be my friend.

I had my first relationship when I was about 18. It was a long distance relationship and I saw him only a few times a year, which was probably why our relationship lasted for as long as it did. I learned how to care for someone. I learned how to be intimate. I could cope with meet ups that were infrequent, and in the meantime we talked on the internet, which was fine. In the beginning, it was sort of exciting because I'd never had a boyfriend before and I liked this young man a lot. He appeared to be quiet and sweet and a bit like me. For several months we got on really well, regardless - or maybe because - of the distance between us. We were both shy, both hard working, and we both loved animals. What he did not know was just how socially awkward I was, how aloof I had the capability of being, and how much I preferred time on my own rather than being with other people. Vice versa, I didn't realise just how sociable he was. He was shy and I made the assumption he was also an introvert but this was not the case, as I found out later.

It never really struck me before but, reading this over makes me realise quite easily how 'false' long distance relationships can be. When I saw him, I only saw the sides he wanted to show me. Because he knew I was quiet and shy, he probably thought that it was better for him to display those qualities of his own. But I missed out on seeing his other side. I probably loved my long distance vision of him. In reality, that vision was not real.

Eventually he moved to London, primarily to go to university but also to be closer to me - and this was when the cracks in our relationship really started to show. The day he moved in to his university residence, he wanted me to go over to see him and help him unpack. I refused to do so, because I just could not bear the stress of having to be around lots of students, many of who would be starters and I imagined a bit hyper with their new freedom and independence away from parents. I think his views on me changed after that. He started to believe I was cruel and cold. I would not attend the parties he invited me to, not even his birthday meal out in a restaurant. It was so hard to explain to him my reasons why. I mentioned Asperger's Syndrome occasionally but, at the time, I didn't have a diagnosis so I suppose he took it with a pinch of salt.

The relationship ended quite soon after he started at university. I suppose the increased time together meant we were both able to see each other's true personality. I loved him so much, but it wasn't enough. I was not able to change who I was, Alis with her Asperger's Syndrome. Intellectually, I wanted to be a part of all the things he did with his friends. But in my heart and my soul, I did not - and I knew I could never be. **I just could not be a neurotypical girl**. It was a painful breakup.

If you look at this another way, a long distance relationship could be the best kind for an Aspie. You get to see your partner infrequently and, when you do see them, you'll probably only see the parts you love about them. When you are apart, they can do all the neurotypical things they want to do and you don't have to be a part of it. Would you like this?

This man had a big influence on my life. I learned a lot of life lessons from him; and *because* of him I imagine I'd otherwise be more innocent and vulnerable than I am now. I do not see him anymore, we have not spoken since the day we split up.

It was only at the beginning of my twenties that I realised that it was okay to be a bit different in today's world. I began to **embrace** my unique personality, rather than suppress it, to try and fit in more with others. The longer I wore my normal mask, the more my personality was suppressed, and there was always a huge emotional price to pay during some terrible episodes of suicidal thoughts, depression, panic attacks, and nervous breakdowns as a teenager.

Over the duration of university, I really grew up and started to find myself. By my fourth and final year, I was nearly totally free of my normal mask. People had accepted me by that time. Perhaps it was because they were older, or because the variety of people at university was just so great.

5.
My Life at Home

Animals

I've grown up around animals, my family always had pets. First we had rabbits, some cats and a dog; then we had more cats, more rabbits, guinea pigs and hamsters; and now we have seven cats and a hamster and we also look after other people's dogs. I've always felt I "obsessively" love and care for them and have always felt a strong bond with animals compared to people. I am absolutely distraught when a pet dies. I feel I have a natural sense of how an animal is feeling. Whenever I go to someone's house, the first thing I do is greet the family pet. Other people are surprised because their normally very timid or shy pet will warm to me immediately.

I really, totally and intensely love animals. They are my friends. Cats are my favourite. I have an enormous attachment to one of our cats, a seal colourpoint Ragdoll called Twinkle, who is totally mine and as besotted with me as I am with her. I'm sure I love her as much as a mother would love her child. Twinkle knows when I'm upset and will snuggle with me for as long as it takes until I am better.

My cats take up all my attention. I love being around them and feel happy in their company. I love cuddling, brushing, feeding and playing with them. Having a pet gives me something to get up for every day; they are dependent on us!

I love how animals experience life. They make it so simple. I watch dogs in the park sometimes, and it's like their only objective is to have fun and play with one another. It doesn't matter if one of the dogs is a groomed princess-like Poodle and the other an old, muddy mongrel. There are no barriers between them - they just are - and they just do what dogs do, no questions asked. Animals also live very much in the present, they don't seem to worry about yesterday or tomorrow. Instead, they are able to live happily in the moment, whatever they are doing. I have learned a lot from animals. If I think more about the now, and less about the 'what ifs' of the past and the future, I am much less anxious. Here is a related quote from the Koran:

'How many animals do not carry their own provision! God provides for them and for you. He is Alert, Aware.' (Islam. Koran. 26.60)

Pets can be really helpful for children and adults with AS. They are highly therapeutic and teach responsibility and maturity. Just simply being with or stroking an animal provides mental and learning benefits.

Stimming

A lot of people with autism do [what is known as] 'stimming' to relax or reassure ourselves, particularly in times of anxiety or stress. Stimming can be anything from rocking on our chair, flapping our hands or jiggling our knees. My stims are 'tactile', which means that they relate to touch and feeling. When I was little, I stimmed on my dog's ears. I've had a cuddly toy koala bear ever since I was a baby and I stroke him in the same place every night (his ear is looking quite worn out now). I also caress my fingers and the palms of my hands very lightly because the feeling is just amazing. I really enjoy it, I do it all the time and it makes me feel relaxed.

Stimming is good, so long as it's appropriate. It's our way of coping with stressful situations. If you are going somewhere you know will be stressful for the AS, suggest they take something with them to help them relax. In my case, this could be my koala bear. This is a good tip for stims that use physical things.

Emotional immaturity

I've heard that people with Asperger's Syndrome mature several years later than others. I've also read that people with AS don't "come into themselves" until their mid-twenties, so it makes sense to describe ourselves as "late developers."

A child or young adult with AS is quite often very immature, naive and vulnerable. Be aware of this and take special attention so they remain in a safe castle! Be an uncritical role model - advise but don't lecture or preach.

I've always noticed and found it really fascinating how I can be so mature in some aspects of life but then so immature in others. I often describe myself as being either a 10 year old or a 50 year old, but never in between. I have that "wise mind, youthful spirit" persona.

When I was a teenager, it was a huge struggle to actually be a teenager.

In many ways, I was still a little girl. In other ways, I was far older. I didn't care about teen crazes and clothing styles. It felt natural to me to not comb my hair, have the same haircut for years, and play with Barbie dolls in my teens.

There is a big difference in the maturity levels of my non-spectrum sister and I and, if they don't know, people often assume that my sister is the older one - both because of her looks and her behaviour. She's really grown up and independent and it's her short-term goal to move out of our family home. My goal is to always stay! As a freelance makeup artist, she's always travelling and going to new places. Recently she moved away and lived in Kent for 4 weeks to work. In my eyes, she makes it look so easy (and fun) to just get in her car and drive or take the train into London. I look at her and observe the way she meets and talks to new people. There's no real "effort," she really is just a genuinely warm, chatty, friendly person! I'm astounded how much she's able to do; the energy that must be required to be social, busy and 'on the go' all the time is just beyond me. Even when not working, she's always going out with her friends and always busy doing something. She's the opposite of me - she seems to get more bored and unhappy being on her own, whereas I get unhappy being with others. The difference is even more pronounced because she is an extrovert.

People who meet me for the first time tend to be very surprised when they find out my age (they think I am much younger); but after getting to know me, I'm told I am quite wise, mature and sensible for my age. Even though I'm 24, I get asked to show ID all the time. I look young; I have the Asperger's Syndrome "cherubic face," and my emotional maturity is probably several years behind. I don't really know how to dress, or how to have long romantic relationships.

Don't compare siblings in a critical way and don't be disappointed because they've turned out differently to one another. The beauty is in the fact that every person is different and their uniqueness should be embraced.

Some of the things I love doing are: reading children's books, doing newspaper rounds, drawing cartoon characters, and watching animated movies. I'm not really interested in moving out of home, buying a car, having a family or paying the bills. My parents and I have an ongoing joke I'm a ten year old (sometimes as old as fourteen, on a "mature day.") I'd say that up until I was about 20, I still had childish tantrums; I think the emotional overload combined with hormonal changes of growing up was just too much.

When I look and hear about other people my age, particularly other women, I feel really "alien." I don't see anything I have in common with them. I am linked to several people from university on my Facebook profile and I feel very different when I read some of their posts. One girl got a job immediately after graduating and it seemed like she didn't think twice about moving all the way to Brighton, leaving her family behind. I think now she's living with her long-term partner. Another boy just got married, I saw his wedding pictures. This is just unbelievable to me; I can't relate to them at all. These people are my age and yet I feel so much younger. I can't begin to imagine doing all the things they do. I still go to the doctor with my mum, go on holiday with my parents, and my dad pays my mobile phone bills.

> Remember that people with AS mature later than NTs. Be patient with your adolescent as they begin the transition into adulthood. We may not yet be ready to move away from home but you can still work with us to set up house rules and responsibilities. Don't compare us to other children the same age.

Thoughts on living independently

Even though I'm becoming more independent, I'm fairly certain that if I had to live on my own, I'd find it hard. I already have trouble remembering to do all those little things that, as people in the Western world, we have to do:

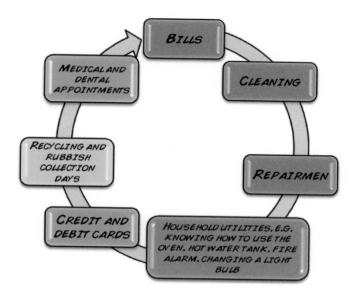

If you don't do these things they can quickly build up and get out of control, which can lead to an AS melt- or shutdown. It's a good idea to create habits that settle these things.

I am aware of most of these things and understand they are important, but it is a big effort to do them - and more effort means more energy expended:

At present, I am doing well living with my parents. Despite the problems, I am very good at managing my income, expenses and generally very good at saving money. I have a weekly spending budget which I stick to. My parents deal with the bills and my mum ensures all my medical history and appointments are organised in a folder. We have a family calendar which I find it helpful to write things on. It is hard knowing when to change my bed sheets; I can go many weeks without doing this and only change them because I know I'm supposed to.

It's no big deal for NTs and ASs to try and live in harmony. The big deal is trying not to get stressed out over minor things that mean a lot to the AS. For example, eating bananas. I don't like the smell of bananas! My dad goes in the garden and we laugh about it.

Even though I like my own space, I would not choose to live alone. If I ever did move out, it would be to live with a very special person - one who could help me with doing normal chores without overwhelming me.

They might also find it hard and restrictive living with me, for example no bananas, no loud noise after 8.00pm and no house parties. The AS isn't easy to live with, but nor is the NT, when they are together. A balance needs to be found.

Worries about abandonment

One of the things I've done to try and learn to cope with my depression has been to attend a course about 'Mindfulness.' Mindfulness is a technique that involves meditation and awareness methods to help combat stress and promote good physical and mental health. There were only a handful of people in my group, and the course took place over eight weeks. Despite my Asperger's Syndrome, I felt quite comfortable talking to the group members. I wonder if that's because I felt less "vulnerable" in their company, because I knew they were vulnerable too? We were all there for the same reason after all - to learn how to cope better with all the challenges in the world.

In some of the sessions we were invited to talk about our experiences. I talked to someone about something on one occasion and she responded with something that really clicked with me and I've never forgotten. She suggested that a lot of my feelings were worries of abandonment and being left on my own. I'd never thought of it that way. It was a revelation to me to think about how a lot of my problems might be caused by my abandonment fears.

I've had a really positive upbringing, so the idea of feeling "scared" of being abandoned is a bit of a strange one to me. A lot of people's problems seem to come from their childhood, but I've never been abandoned and I've always had lots of love and attention from the family around me.

But even so, despite my happy childhood, I still have terrible worries about abandonment and I've had them for a long time. At 24 I am still clingy and needy for my parents and I feel totally distraught the times they go away on holiday on their own. I don't like being so attached to them; I know it upsets them that I feel so miserable when they do their own thing without me. I just feel like I can't handle the world on my own.

When I was little, I used to scream and cry when my mum left me alone at nursery school. In primary school, I'd run out of school all the time. I hated her leaving me on my own. I had so many behavioural/temper outbursts, seemingly for no real reason at all. I'll always remember one time my parents took my sister and I to an arts and crafts club for an afternoon. My parents thought I would like it but I really didn't want to be there. I became withdrawn and did not play with the other children. I stood on my own by the front door. It was torturous and I was very unhappy.

> Work out whether your child is simply being naughty or is genuinely distressed. They might be having a meltdown.

As far as relationships go, all the times I've ever "liked" someone I'm always so scared they're going to give up on me that I'd rather not even try to make a relationship successful. Abandonment makes me feel completely destroyed, which is an **unbelievable** hurt. My feelings of being abandoned are really hard to let go of. I fear they have stopped some relationships progressing as they could have because of my worries and constant anxieties that a partner will get sick of my "quirks." I fear my worries have caused my parents enormous amounts of unnecessary stress.

My parents sometimes want to go on holiday or out for dinner without me being there. I have adapted to this and try really hard to let them have their own time. I know they still love me. I try to let them have their own space, without them having to ask me for it. I know they're coming home soon!

An endless list of questions

My mother is a kind and patient woman. Because human beings are so illogical, she has to answer all the questions that I have, which the world just cannot answer. Every day, she is bombarded with my questions about **why** or **how** something could have happened. I am under the impression that other people can just shrug these sort of questions off, or perhaps they don't ask them at all. But I am always questioning and I cannot stop thinking about something unless it has been answered for me.

Some examples are described on the next page.

ORANGE HANDS

Due to the amount of carrots I eat, my hands sometimes have a very slight orange tinge. To a distant eye, it just looks like I am very tanned!

Sometimes people will say something to me, such as "Your hands are very orange. What is that?"

I find this quite invasive. I do not make remarks on others, so I do not understand why they feel that they have the right to question my own appearance.

I do not understand why it is considered acceptable for people to ask about my skin colour, yet apparently it is considered unacceptable for me to, for example, ask why somebody is overweight.

For this one, my mum explained that the reason it is more acceptable for people to comment on orange hands, is because it's more unusual. It's still annoying, but I sort of understand this. She also said that it is okay to tell people that they are putting on weight, but only really if they are family or very close friends. And you should comment sensitively.

DELIVERIES

I was expecting something to be delivered in the post. On that day, I had to be out of the house. So I left a big note on the doorstep that said, "Urgently needed today! Please leave package with any neighbour." In addition, I used the courier company's online delivery service to check the box that said 'Give permission for our driver to leave your package with the neighbour, if you know you're going to be out.'

Now, in my mind, there was no possible way that the package would not be there for me when I got home. I had implemented all the correct steps to ensure that it would be deposited safely.

When I got home, there was a note from the courier company which said, 'Sorry, your parcel has been returned to the delivery office because you were out.'

I was distraught. It did not make sense to me how on earth this could have happened. I did not understand why the courier company even bothered having an online delivery service with "leave with neighbour" option if they weren't going to use it. Plus, my note had clearly stated in very big black letters that this package was "urgently needed today." I had no idea how this could have happened. I was so upset and so confused. My world had fallen apart.

The parcel arrived the next day.

My mum agreed with me that the courier's service was somewhat flawed. She suggested that either the man had not seen my note, or that the courier's computer system was faulty and he had not seen my "Yes, it's okay to leave with neighbour" box that was ticked. In this case, we found out what really happened - which was great! As the man dropped off the parcel the next day, he explained that he had tried every neighbour yesterday, but no one had been in. Finally, I understood. It all made sense. And I could get over it.

PAPER ROUNDS

I deliver newspapers every day. At 5 o' clock in the morning I arrive at the shop to collect my newspaper rounds, before I go off to deliver them.

There are a total of ten newspaper rounds, numbered from 1 to 10. I do two of them (round 6 and round 8).

The other kids arrive at 6.30am to collect their newspapers. I arrive early at 5.00am because I am awake anyway and like to get my job finished and complete so that I can get on with my own day. Also, Round 6 consists of commercial places, such as hotels, which like to receive their newspapers early for their guests. If I delivered the papers at 6.30am, it would be too late for them.

I am always extremely confused when I arrive at the shop to find that my boss has started to get the newspaper rounds ready, but he has organised them in sequential order, which means that when I arrive, rounds 1 and 2 tend to already be complete - he is getting 3 ready but only when he sees me arrive does it occur to him to start on rounds 6 and 8.

This confuses me so much because I end up having to wait an extra ten minutes for him to have rounds 6 and 8 ready. If he had prepared them, then I would've been in and out of the shop very quickly - the papers would be delivered very quickly and early on. Surely that means less stress for him too?

I have asked him many, many times, if he could please do rounds 6 and 8 first. But he will only seem to do this if I am there in person to remind him. If I arrive early enough, before he has started organising the rounds, he will do rounds 6 and 8 first. But if I come in slightly later, it is guaranteed that rounds 1, 2 and maybe even 3, 4 and 5 have already been done... BEFORE my own.

It does not make sense to me, because the other rounds do not get delivered until 6.30am.

PAPER ROUNDS CONTINUED...

So, on the mornings that this happens, I ask my mum just how this situation could happen, time and time again. She agrees with me that it doesn't make sense. Her answers to how this could happen are, "Because he's human, he just forgets," or "Because he's the boss and can do what he wants," or "Perhaps you should start going in to the shop at 6.30am instead? Then they would always be ready for you." The best answer she has suggested is, "Sometimes people have to do things in certain ways, else they make mistakes. Perhaps he just has to prepare them in sequential order, otherwise he feels worried he'll make mistakes." She has also suggested that I ask him to replace the numbers "6" and "8" with "1" and "2." If my paper rounds were made to be the first ones, then perhaps it would be better...

Discussing this situation with my mum has made me feel better - she has given me possible reasons and, although I will probably never find out the true reason for my boss's actions, she has provided me with an adequate amount of closure that allows me to get on with things...

You might notice that your Aspie son or daughter asks lots of questions - questions that might seem meaningless to you. They are probably not being nosey or trying to annoy you deliberately - they are most likely just trying to understand a world which is so, SO confusing to them. Please do your best to answer their questions, no matter how small. If you don't have an answer, I prefer it when my mum is honest and just says, "I don't know."

6.
Me

An observer in life

I often consider myself to be an observer in life, rather than a participant. I have heard that lots of other people with Asperger's Syndrome have a similar experience. This is a quote from a lady with Asperger's Syndrome, which describes my own feelings very well:

'As a consequence of this condition, I believe I am a bewildered stranger in our social world.' (Lianne Holliday Wiley[8], 1999)

Throughout my life there have been periods where I've felt very disconnected and aloof from other people. These feelings are not present all of the time, but they are present most of the time I am out in a public place. I love observing all kinds of human behaviour and emotion. I think that it is because of this intense interest in observing, that I have a fair amount of knowledge about the behaviour of others. There is such a thing as 'Theory of Mind' which means intuitively knowing the meaning or intention of another person. Over the course of my life I think I have learned an adequate quantity of Theory of Mind, unless of course it's just my instinct? Certainly I get confused sometimes, but I can feel the warmth of a smile or the meaning of a glance. However, sometimes it's hard to imagine what they are thinking.

Although I often feel disconnected from others, I believe I am connected to the world, just not in a social sort of way. I am very aware of the little things, such as patterns or subtleties in the world around me. Everything around me is like a different piece in a jigsaw puzzle.

I love writing stories or making up stories in my head. I am able to very accurately capture the essence of a person - their looks, mannerisms, their language, their whole "being." I am often complimented on the depth of my characters in my stories. I am good at writing creatively, writing scientific reports and letters, however when I write about myself, the language is rather formal and odd.

In truth, I think there is such a thing as thinking too much. Ruminating, particularly about negative things, is unhealthy for me. My mind never

8 Holliday Wiley, L (1999). Pretending to be Normal. London: Jessica Kingsley Publishers. 9.

sleeps - I am always examining my surroundings, looking for reasons, or meanings in everything. I feel that this has its pros - perhaps I notice more than other people, but a big drawback is that I am less able to use intuition - I have to work it out. Sometimes it feels that if I just said "yes" or "okay" rather than endlessly analyse a process over and over again, much more would be resolved and I would feel a lot less anxious. Even the smallest things cause me to go through an endless list of possibilities, eventualities, problems, benefits and worries. It is no wonder I am anxious all the time. Everything is confusing because I can't just work out the answer. Too much thinking can even make me cry.

Desire for knowledge/Needing to know things/'Scripting'

For every planned situation, my head contains every single consequence, outcome, alternative and possibility. In an unplanned situation none of these thoughts exist, so they have to be constructed, from scratch. This takes up energy. My existence runs on a very complicated thought-process. It is no wonder I am exhausted all the time. "Simple" decisions have big emotional consequences. Scenarios that have not been planned for, such as finding out the gym has unexpectedly closed due to a power cut, or that my favourite food item is out of stock, have the potential to disrupt an entire day's routine - which can make me feel extremely anxious and upset.

It bothers me when people don't explain why they are doing things. I need a full explanation for everything. I can become very confused by the actions of someone and so I am always asking "why?" Facts, reasons and rationale in conversation are incredibly important, otherwise I can feel very confused and distressed. Here is an example:

THE 11 O' CLOCK MASSAGE

My friend is on holiday from university and has a lot of free time during the day. We often arrange for him to come over and give me a massage at a convenient time for me.

One Thursday in the early morning I asked him if he could massage me later on that day. He responded, "of course. What time?" and I replied, "11.00-12.00pm." He told me that he was busy at that time. I told him that I was busy for the rest of the day and only had a free slot at 11.00-12.00pm. I asked him what he had planned to be doing between 11 and 12. He said "I need to do some admin work." I then asked him what he would be doing in the afternoon. He replied, "nothing, I'm free this afternoon." This confused me because I wondered why he could not move his admin work to the afternoon (usually he is very flexible and accommodating). When I asked him this, his response was "I just like to do it at that time." I did not find this to be a good enough reason, I could not understand and felt extremely frustrated and confused.

When I probed him later on, he told me that he had arranged a phone call for 11am and that was why he had been unavailable at that time. I then understood why he was so persistent he could not see me at 11.00am.

I wish he could have told me about this pre-arranged phone call at the beginning, it would have made me understanding instead of feeling intensely confused and frustrated.

Do you notice how it never occurred to me to rearrange my day to accommodate him? Even if I had thought of that (or if he had suggested it), I could not have changed my plans - my whole day would be ruined.

Only when I receive explanations and reasons do I obtain closure. When I obtain closure, I feel safer, less anxious, more secure, and more enlightened. Suddenly the world is a much more comfortable place. The following situation gives an example of exactly what I mean. See if you can understand my thought process and reaction:

THE FAULTY FREEZERS

I regularly buy ice cream from my local supermarket, however the last few times I have been, there have been freezer problems, so ice cream is unavailable. I notified them of this problem. On each occasion I have enquired with a member of staff about why there always seem to be a freezer problem and when it will be resolved. Every single time I am told "Oh I don't know."

I don't understand how different members of staff don't seem to know when the problem will be fixed. They never seem to act on my complaint. This makes me feel extremely distressed. It doesn't make sense to me that this situation isn't taken seriously.

I went back to buy ice cream a couple of weeks later and there were signs all over the freezers saying "faulty." This time I asked another member of staff how long they were going to be like this. He told me that the freezers had always only been temporary ones and were going to be replaced in a few weeks. This now helped to uplift my mood, because he had provided an accurate explanation. I achieved closure that I had not received from the other staff members. The situation no longer bothers me.

As I am writing this situation I am feeling stressed. I am reliving this experience. Wherever possible you have to find a workaround, which causes you less stress. Solutions could be to ask an NT friend to talk to the staff because they would probably find it less stressful. Go to a different store. Order the ice cream online - and recognise that these kind of experiences can be triggers for distress.

I need routine and facts in my life. I always like to know what I'm going to be doing and at exactly what time. I also like to know about what the people close to me will be doing and when. When I was little and my parents went out without me, I always asked them "where are you going?" and "what time will you be back?" Actually, I still do this! I need to know for my own peace of mind. I get very anxious when I don't know what's going to be happening.

> Many NTs embrace change and like trying new things. The AS should understand that some people get excited by not planning and being spontaneous, just as we get excited by planning and scripts.

I also need to know about the actions of somebody else because they can affect my own schedule. For example, I need to know whether my sister is going to be at home in the morning because, if she is, I should lift weights at 1.00pm and not 7.30am in case I wake her. This means that I will need to be doing something different at 7.30am, so to know in advance means I can plan to do that something else.

I think it drives my parents mad that I'm always asking them what they're up to. I'm interested in their lives and like to know when they're going to be at home, because that makes me feel loved and safe. I need to feel secure as the world is so confusing.

> I understand the concept of spontaneity and 'going with the flow' even if I don't apply it myself. When I ask my mum what she's up to she sometimes says, "I don't know, will just see how I feel and what I fancy doing!" It drives me mad! :) But I appreciate her honesty and have learned to accept that she enjoys the unpredictability of life, whereas I like things to be predictable.

There is a good description of the need to plan:

'"Scripting": the golden rule in autism. We need every second of every minute of every hour scripted.' (Deborah Lipsky[9], 2011)

I know that, in my head, every day I have these so-called "scripts" of how things in the day are going to happen. This script provides schedules and clarity for me, the person with Asperger's Syndrome, but once the rest of the world is involved, the script often goes off track. I like knowing things, with minutiae, to the second, and if I have a script it ensures that all these things are known. Without a script, things become unknown,

---

9 Lipsky, D (2011). From Anxiety to Meltdown: How Individuals on the Autism Spectrum Deal with Anxiety, Experience Meltdowns, Manifest Tantrums, and How You Can Intervene Effectively. London: Jessica Kingsley Publishers. 26.

and this can cause great stress and anxiety.

It is often noted that people with Asperger's Syndrome crave control.

'The nature of autism is the brain's desire to keep the world the same.' (Mark Bowers[10], 2009)

Meltdowns and shutdowns are almost always caused by an external stimulus in the environment. Our immediate environment is very uncontrollable, primarily because of other people. Some examples may include train delays, doctors running late, a teacher not turning up, etc.

Whenever I have an appointment with my doctor, I am almost always seen some time after my scheduled appointment time. Even when they say they are running on schedule I can be seen ten minutes late, and I usually end up waiting a lot longer just because that's what they think is normal!

Why is it that, if I am five minutes late (unlikely, but just to prove a point) to my 9.00am appointment, I lose the appointment altogether and have to book another one? Yet, when my doctor is late I am still expected to be available to attend. It is socially acceptable for me to be seen at 9.30am because she is running late, but not 9.05am if I'd been late. In addition, that extra thirty minutes of waiting time has now shifted the plans in my day back by thirty minutes. Everything in my script has changed, which makes me feel extremely anxious.

Do you notice that my preoccupation is about how it affects me? It never occurs to me there may be a good reason for the doctor running late, e.g. another patient needed extra time.

It is also common for me to meet someone at our meeting place or rendezvous, rather than for us to go there together. For example, if there was an agenda to meet for a cup of tea at 11.00am or to see a movie due to start at 11.00am, I would much rather get there on my own so that I keep to my script, no matter what the other person is doing. My friend and I meet regularly in our local cafe, yet we each take our own bikes

10 Bowers, M. (2009). Scripting and the autistic veil. Available: http://drbowers.wordpress.com/2009/10/16/scripting-and-the-autistic-veil/. Last accessed 16th Sep 2013.

and travel there separately, despite living as neighbours. I do not want to be committed to someone else's schedule or script. Many things could go wrong - they could get a flat tyre, suddenly there might be a phone call just as they're about to leave the house, they leave their bike lock at home and have to go back for it etc. I want to be reliant upon myself and not someone else.

I am very easily confused when things are not correct. For example, there is a supermarket which states on the signs outside, 'Open 7 Days a Week 06:00-12:00am.' This is fine - it is clear. However, what is **not** clear is the line underneath, which states, 'Open Until 22:00 on Sundays.' I find this unbelievably confusing, because the second line contradicts the first line.

I also feel extremely confused when I see signs on shop doors, such as 'Back in 2 minutes,' when the sign does not state what time it was written. Or what about the boards you sometimes see outside pubs, that say 'Live music tonight?' I do not know which "tonight" they are referring to - often, the board is left up for several days.

Needing to be mothered

I tend to get on better with older people than people my own age and, as a child, I remember enjoying the company and attention of adults. Whenever I saw friends, I enjoyed talking to their parents. Two of my closest friends now are women aged around fifty years old, with whom I have very strong connections. It's my natural instinct to want to be very close to women of an age that they could be my mother. Certainly I'm really (probably overly) attached to my own mum but I'm happy to be "mothered" by anyone. I think I must emit a very innocent and juvenile persona to the world because, older women seem to want to look after me as well. Once, I considered having a romantic relationship with an older woman simply because I wanted her to take care of me.

76

> I have heard that people with AS tend to get on much better with people older than them. If you have trouble finding friends, consider meeting up with someone older than you. They are often less judgemental, more comfortable in themselves and worry less about things like looks and being part of the crowd. They often have a more mature mindset and an open outlook on life.

Whenever I make appointments with anyone, my preference is to always see a 50+ year old woman. I also prefer her to be big and cuddly because it makes me feel loved and safe! My doctor and acupuncturist have been like this. I guess I always just need to feel looked after because I feel unable, or too vulnerable, to cope with things on my own.

Even though I'm 24, the rare occasions that I'm part of a group, if someone tells a joke or uses "adult" innuendo, it's not uncommon for someone else to jump in and tell me to cover my ears or jokingly remind the others that "young Alis" is present!

I am naive in the sense that I can be easily led, simply because I have the belief that most people are kind and are not looking to take advantage of me. If I am having a conversation with someone who is a strong or dominant character then I can have a lot of difficulty holding on to my point of view. Sometimes I'll even start to believe the other person's view over mine, simply because they have the ability to build a better argument or foundation. My dad has often told me not to speak to companies that market mobile phones etc. via the telephone, because salesmen can bend my views and make me lose my ground.

Easily offended

I've described myself as "emotionally immature" and a part of this is my innocence. For my age, I am innocent. Sometimes my sister talks about things I have no idea about and she chuckled at me when I learned that 'MILF' meant 'Mother I'd Like to F*!$. She was also the one who advised me about sex.

I really, really, hate swearing, alcohol and smoking. I wonder if it's because I have Asperger's Syndrome that I feel so strongly about this, or are they just quirks of my personality? At school, I remember hearing that many of my classmates enjoyed a bit of alcohol and smoking. Even though I was never coerced into either of these, I still never had the slightest inclination to try them. I just never had that youthful, experimental desire that all the other teenagers seemed to have. It bothers me the way that drinking alcohol is so regularly publicised and almost "praised" in society and in the media. I don't know whether people are being sarcastic and playful, or whether they are serious when they talk about alcohol, for example, about having had too much to drink last night.

I do not like swearing. It might sometimes have its place in situations of extreme anger, but regular use of swear words in everyday life is just always inappropriate. Just today I heard on the radio that the average person swears sixteen times a day! I do not want to hear people swearing when I am out in public taking a walk or sitting in a coffee bar. It makes me extremely uncomfortable. There is no reason to swear, the words are extremely ugly and rude. Teenagers are the worst, for some reason they think it's cool to add a swear word to every sentence. Maybe it is the rigidity that comes with having Asperger's Syndrome that has made me strictly believe that swearing is impolite and wrong. When people deviate from these societal 'rules,' it can make me feel distressed. Sometimes I wonder whether it was my adherence to rules and my strong differentiation between right and wrong, which made me seem older than everybody else in my attitude, whilst also being innocent and naive. I remember once at school, a classmate asked me, "do you ever do anything wrong, even at home?"

I don't think that my strong dislike for swearing, alcohol and smoking is specific to having Asperger's Syndrome. But I think what it illustrates is that I do not always fit in socially. A lot of socialising, particularly when you are young, seems to involve these things. Forcing yourself to fit in to uncomfortable situations can highlight your differences which in turn, can increase stress and sadness.

I do not like to watch films above an age 12 rating because I get very upset and disturbed seeing portrayals of crime, violence, sex or death. Several years ago I made the biggest mistake of watching a thriller film with an 18 rating (I was young and bored one summer holiday) and all these years later I am still disturbed by some of the scenes which I can still picture extremely vividly in my mind. I don't like to hear vulgar language in films. I find it really hard to follow the storylines of a lot of films, particularly when they're real action/non-animated. I am frequently unable to understand their content.

My favourite things to watch would be light family comedies or fantasies, but mostly animations. I like watching things that make me feel happy or uplifted, and I like things with simple storylines. Children's animations often have just one 'good guy' and one 'baddie' and the good guy always wins! I like it kept simple...

I think I have very "soft" views of the world. By this I mean that I believe most people are kind. I try my best to avoid the news because hearing about the bad things that happen makes me really sad and uncomfortable. I'd rather be ignorant of bad things; I don't want to believe there are bad people, murder, crime and rape; and if I don't see them, then I don't have to believe they happen. This is my way of protecting myself. I might be very capable academically, but I still have the emotional characteristics of a child.

Unpleasant scenes or words - fantasy or otherwise - remain a vivid picture in my mind and can be recalled at any time in the future. These pictures upset me greatly, so I have learned to be cautious with the media.

A couple of years ago I reconnected on Facebook with someone I'd known at primary school. I remember vividly this girl as being sweet, lovable and very sensitive. She was a lovely little girl. We met up, having not seen each other for around 13 years! I couldn't believe how much she'd changed - I still felt so young and innocent and she was clearly now a grown woman. She told me that she had had intercourse with twelve people and I couldn't believe it. In my mind, she was still that sweet, innocent 9 year old! But it was me - I was still that innocent 9 year old.

I just couldn't relate to her at all, even though we'd had lots in common when we were children. Our meet up showed me how different we were. I wondered whether I should be living a similar lifestyle.

I do not always like it when people tease me, even though most of the time it's done in fondness. For example, once a friend of mine commented on my clothing. She said, "I never see you wear anything else!" I felt self-conscious and embarrassed for a long time after. Because she was my friend, I was able to tell her that she had made me feel self-conscious. She apologised and said she had not meant to hurt me, it was just an observation, not a criticism or a personal attack. My parents know to tell me they are just teasing, when they are teasing me. Otherwise I can easily feel upset.

A strong sense of individuality

Although I'm very attached to my parents, it's deep rooted inside me that it's best to be wholly self-sufficient in the world. Unfortunately it is a characteristic of being human that we may let down or disappoint others - we are not robots! I love my family and I trust them to keep me safe and know they will always provide for me; but to the rest of the world, I strive to be a self-contained, self-controlled being with my own ideas, my own ethics and my own values. I always take my own antibacterial wipes out when I go to cafes because if the staff are busy, I do not have to rely on them to clean my table. Instead, I can quickly do it myself and get straight on with my work.

I have decided that, to obtain security and harmony (my life goals), it is best to try and only depend on myself. I get very hurt by people letting me down and so try to avoid chances of this happening, whenever I can. I let people down too, but I think that I feel much more hurt than they do. I can shut down easily which may lead to depression.

It is a glorious feeling to be content in myself without succumbing to the realms of "normal" society.

This diagram on the next page shows some of my quirks which make up my individuality:

Another quirk may be that I prefer to be at home on Friday and Saturday nights writing my book, whereas the majority of people my age go out clubbing or to the pub with their friends. I also have a strong eye for missing commas or apostrophes and I will notice if they are missing immediately.

The world is not "ideally" built for those of us on the autistic spectrum. I have a lot of problems with the world and I can so easily feel confused and lost. I am driven by logic and reasoning but the non-autistic world is very chaotic. I need to know reasons and rules for everything before I act upon something. If something is done in a certain way, I need to know why so that it will make sense. If it is too vague, it's not an acceptable reason in my mind and I will struggle to understand or comply with the "rules."

I can only feel safe in a world with order and rationality - when it's not, I feel anxious and unsettled. I find it really hard to understand - and have patience for - people who are unable to provide me with adequate explanations. Consequently, romantic relationships are really hard for me.

I do not understand it when a reason given for something is "Because I say so" or "Because we just can't!"

> Although I like rituals and scripts in my life, I do not like social rituals and scripts. I prefer social rituals to be flexible and on my own terms because I don't know how my social energy levels will be at that time. Some people might feel that everything is always on my terms, but I can't help being this way...

Unfortunately (and confusingly), I also "battle" my independence with a deep yearning to connect with other people and maybe even love someone. So even though I want to be self-reliant, I'm also very aware that it's hard to cope on my own.

In the end, I want to be able to love someone who meets my criteria. I would then be able to give up some of my independence and enjoy a happy relationship.

> As the NT partner this can be really hard because they want the AS to open up and let them in. It's an issue of trust. The AS should learn that, once they've found that special person, it's OK to trust them and know they never intend to hurt you. It's a 'chicken and egg' situation because if the AS closes up and shuts them out, the NT will never get better at meeting their needs. The AS will learn to trust their NT partner but it will take time. In the meantime, the NT must be understanding. The AS typically desires solidity, stability and reliability and this type of relationship will take time to build and progress. AS/NT relationships are often very hard but they can also be the most special and meaningful.
>
> It may appear that the NT has to make extra effort to make everything work. In return, the AS will probably be one of the most straightforward, faithful, honest and loyal partners they will ever have.

Sexuality and asexuality

Being a teenage girl in a mixed-sex school was really hard because unlike the other girls my age, I didn't 'fancy' boys. Sometimes it felt as though it was only boys and "who has a crush on who" that were always on their minds. As an observer, I could see that these girls were experiencing changes in behaviour. They were becoming increasingly interested in the opposite sex, but I was not. It was a very strange feeling.

> A lot of people on the autistic spectrum are asexual. Passion may be lacking in the relationship, which could be hard for the NT. Partners may want to explore other ways of being intimate, e.g. massage.

I've spent a lot of my life being around, and observing, other people. Even through watching soaps and dramas on the T.V., reading, and listening to the radio, I've learned a lot about human behaviour. I can't seem to get away from the fact that our culture constantly communicates to us that falling in love and being with someone, are two really, really important things. Consequently, it seems to me that the 'aims' of a lot of people revolve around meeting others. I've always felt really uncomfortable, if I hear someone say something like "I need to find a guy/girl tonight."

> Similar sayings are "I want to hook up with someone" or "I want to get laid." My NT friend told me that these phrases are supposedly said in humour and jest, but he admits that there's often also some truth to them.

I don't ever actively seek out friends or take part in socialising, but if I do find someone who happens to share some interests, I'm more likely to enjoy building a relationship with them.

My first kiss was ridiculous. I didn't know how to do it and I told him this. He laughed at me and said "how can you not know how to kiss?" and then he spent a long time trying to teach me! Kissing just didn't feel natural or enjoyable, how I imagined it would be for other people.

I have had intercourse several times and not really enjoyed it. The sexual attraction just hasn't ever existed, except in my first relationship, but I think that was probably more because of the novelty of first love. I simply don't have any sexual feelings. I don't fancy people or have fantasies. I don't know what a libido feels like and I can't actually "tell" when I'm aroused, usually my partner has to tell me.

I don't understand how some people seem to need to have regular sex. Once I read somewhere that one of the benefits of being in a relationship was the opportunity to enjoy regular sex. It just does not cross my mind as something I ever need to do! Honestly, I don't really like sex, but occasionally I might enjoy certain aspects of it (but these feelings are fluid and inconsistent).

I can understand why other people like to do it. But I never yearn for or desire it and probably wouldn't even notice if I didn't do it for the rest of my life.

I don't find human beings particularly "aesthetically pleasing." In my eyes, we are very limby, hairless, abnormal-looking mammals. I see beauty in a shiny new racing bike, a bouquet of Hyacinth flowers, a barbell, or one of my cats...

I have heard that some people with AS will only be attracted to partners with physical features that meet certain criteria, e.g. blonde hair, symmetric face, looks like Mum etc.

I feel I am sort of unfocused or bisexual but not really interested in sex (does that make any sense at all?). I'm not particularly interested in either sex - a person is a person. I see people more for their personality and who they are, rather than their gender or looks. I could honestly see myself attached to either a man or a woman and if ever there was the smallest chance of sexual intimacy in response to being with someone else, it'd probably be with a woman. I don't know why.

When I have a male partner, although I do find him attractive, I just don't really look at anyone in "that way." I feel it is hard to work out my sexuality because I am a bit indifferent to men and to women. I feel that because we are the same, it is hard to have a preference between men and women. I do not understand heterosexuality, apart from being in a stable relationship from which you can have children.

I often wonder whether there is a real connection between having an autism spectrum disorder and being asexual. Certainly having social struggles reduces the chances of us meeting and connecting with others - but regardless, if the opportunity arose, I imagine that the sensory issues that come with being so close to someone, could be extremely unsettling. Be aware also that, medications such as some antidepressants, can lower your sex drive. If your sex drive is low, think about whether it was low before you started your medication, or whether it has become low as a consequence. You can talk to your GP about changing medication if this is the case.

I enjoy companionship (with some people, sometimes, on my terms), and I would like to find a partner who I could count as "family" one day but it is not a priority for me. I have put time and effort into relationships that end up falling apart. All relationships are challenging but, in my experience, it is the 'mixed' AS/NT relationships that are the hardest ones. I do not have enough energy to try and make my relationships work, when in my heart I know that relationships are not a priority to me. I am not romantically inclined (even more so as I get older). I can no longer relate to being a part of a romantic partnership. I feel that because my social energy tank is limited, I can't afford to expend energy on something that in my heart I don't really want.

Just the thought of regular kissing or prolonged touching is uncomfortable. I have "put up" with sex for the benefit of my partners in the past but, even then, I have to be in a certain state of mind. I go through "states" of having a tolerance for sex, and states of not wanting to be touched at all. I mostly exist in the second mind state, where I just detest, hate, dread, any form of touch, and the idea of sex becomes extremely frightening and disturbing.

Unfortunately I've never found anyone who does truly accept I'm asexual and that I really don't want children. Some of my relationships have ended because I was unable to cope with physical contact and they were unable to cope without it. I find this level of intimacy empty and unrewarding.

Sometimes I wish that the physical aspects of my relationships were more like what other human relationships seem to be. Most NT/NT relationships are more physical. I realise it would be much easier for my NT partner if we could have a more physical relationship.

I am confused about my sexuality. My experience of dating is that it just feels like friendship. I cannot differentiate between loving a friend and being in love with someone. I have love for my friends that feels no different than the love I've had for partners. The only comparison in trying to describe this is to say that, romantic love for me is like trying to describe an elephant to a blind person.

When I was at university, my classmates often spoke about their partners or expressed their visions of future husbands or wives. I didn't crave the same sort of life "experience" that they did. The expectation of a relationship is to be social and participate in kissing and touching, which did not appeal to me.

Sensitive but lacking empathy

I love my family. I'm very attached to and dependent on my parents. But it always confuses me when people feel sad about people they hear about but don't know. I've overhead many conversations and been part of them, where people are expressing emotion for others who were killed in war, drowned or were starved etc. It is sad when others feel pain but, most of the time these things are out of my control. I avoid the news because I don't want to waste energy feeling sad about something over which I have no control and which does not directly affect me or those I love. This has frequently been said to me, "Don't you think it's terrible, what's been going on? Aren't you upset about it?"

And yet bad news about the world upsets me greatly, in a confusing way. I very much live inside my own experiences and something that's happened outside of it that I can't do anything about will not affect me here, now, today. I have trouble relating to and feeling pain about things that I have not personally experienced. Coupled with needing to avoid situations where I will feel emotions may overload me, I can appear oblivious to someone else's distress.

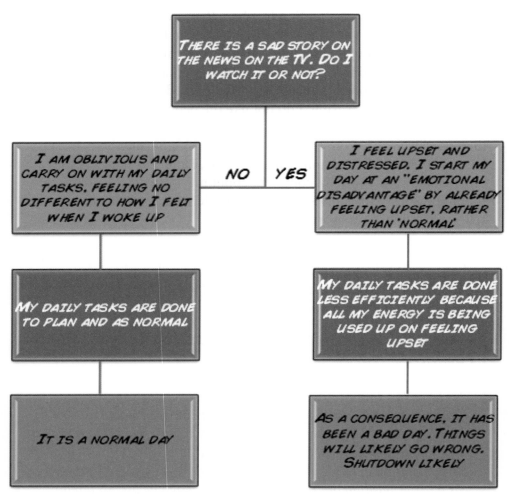

Whilst my lack of response can give the impression that I'm cold or unfeeling, really it's a form of self-protection. My preference is always to be happy over sad. Either feeling can be overwhelming but negative feelings are paralysing. It's confusing that it does not drive me to help others who are hurt. I just feel so, so overwhelmed and so I try to stay oblivious.

I always say that you can be either be happy or sad with an autism spectrum disorder. You have the choice. I choose to be happy, life's a lot nicer this way.

I've been told I can have a black and white view about other people contributing to their misfortunes. Grey is very hard for me. For example if someone bumps into a lamp post, in my mind I think they should have been paying more attention to where they are going. I don't bump into things because I'm always sure to look where I'm going; and I feel it's silly for others not to do likewise. However, that doesn't mean I don't care. When something bigger has happened (perhaps something that's more out of their control), maybe their father died or they lost their job, I am probably overly caring. I do not like the people I care about to feel upset. Unfortunately though, what happens is that I get upset too. I can then quickly switch from trying to help them to ignoring them, because I am overwhelmed. And annoyingly for NTs, I am very sensitive to others making any form of comment about my apparent disinterest or thoughtlessness. My super sensitivity to criticism in addition to my high self-expectations, can overwhelm me.

It's often said that people with AS see the world in "black and white," whereas most NTs see shades of grey. I'm able to intellectually understand shades of grey in challenging situations but my emotional reactions to things are likely to be much more black and white and extreme.

You might find the situation interesting:

VOLUNTARY WORK

My clever, hard working, 29 year old friend was doing some ongoing voluntary work for a well off company. Many times he asked himself whether he was being taken advantage of. When we spoke about it, I just said it how I saw it. In my mind, he was a bright, 29 year old, independent, man living alone in his own house, I was certain there was a better position out there for him. I suggested he ask for a paid position at the company. When the company said no, my friend left the job. He'd appreciated hearing my blunt, unbiased views. Now he has a paid job in a good company, which he is thoroughly enjoying.

As in this case, black and white thinking isn't always bad. NTs often appreciate the rawness of our answers, without the emotional overlay that NTs seem to use. People with AS can often give good, logical advice without being aware of too many different perspectives to resolve.

Too emotionally sensitive

Some people think people with Asperger's Syndrome have no emotion, but actually a lot of us are too sensitive and too emotional. I'm so emotionally sensitive that it's easy for me to become totally consumed in my worries about anxieties, fears, guilt, depression, suicidal moods, loneliness, feeling different and any other intense emotions. Inside I am full of intense chaos. People with Asperger's Syndrome are said to have "unusual world paradigms."

Some emotionally sensitive traits of mine are:

I've never felt comfortable sharing my concerns with other people my age, because I've found they usually don't have the same concerns. Instead, their priorities are more focused on issues of lifestyle (their job, their relationship etc.) and on fitting in with expectation ("what should I wear today?"); but I am more interested in what makes up an individual and the depth of a person. From a young age, I philosophised and challenged many of society's rules and conventions ("why do women have to wear skirts to interviews?", "why do I have to go to school?", "why don't more people recycle?", "how can we abolish cruelty to animals?") which made me feel frustrated, disappointed and isolated.

When I was a teenager I felt depressed because I would endlessly mull over whether life really had any meaning at all. I like this quote:

'Welcome to Planet Asperger, located in a parallel universe where everything seems the same as earth, but nothing actually is.' (R. Young[11], 2009)

I really understand this; I continually experience feelings of being alone. It always feels there's a "gap" between me and someone else. I often feel I am another species and don't always like human beings.

> Many people with Asperger's Syndrome tend to think a lot and at deeper levels. You may ask questions that can't be answered, which can make you feel frustrated or depressed. These can be questions that others rarely ever think about. Other people can accept that life "just is." They accept 'not knowing.' But I know that I am always questioning. Are you?

Even though I'm not a 'people-person' I'm still extremely sensitive and aware of other peoples' emotions. I always want to help people and make them feel better. I've even worked as a carer for the elderly. If someone I love is sad then I am very likely going to be sad with them. I'll worry about them and think about them all the time. When my lovely grandad died, I was heartbroken; but I remember acknowledging that actually most of my hurt was for my granny and how she was going to cope without him after 60+ years of being with him. I hurt so much for her, it was agonising. Yet I could not do what she needed and go to his funeral. I needed to do what I needed to do, which was to stay away. Outwardly it could've seemed unsupportive, but I just could not receive any more of the inescapable agony I was experiencing for a man who loved me and who I loved unconditionally. I was unable to go to the funeral to support my family. I cannot work out whether this is really looking after myself or not thinking of others. I always feel inside that I care deeply about others, but I don't know if this caring is always properly understood or how it might be perceived.

---

11 Young, R (2009). Asperger Syndrome Pocketbook. Hampshire: Teachers' Pocketbooks. 8.

I love my grandparents. I was certainly sad for my gran. But was I also sad because of how this situation was going to affect me? That perhaps Gran was now less able to look after me?

I worry all the time about my mum. She's such a beautiful, loving, kind lady but she works so hard in a mentally demanding and exhausting job. I think about the ways I can make life easier for her, by offering to rub her feet or shoulders, making her a cup of tea or running her a bath for when she gets back from work. But it is often on my terms. Sometimes I may not notice what she needs or if the timing does not suit me I will just say no. For my routine or plans to be disrupted by others is unbearably distressing and I can't function. Sorry.

When my sister and her boyfriend decided to end their 10+ year relationship, I was very sad for her. I didn't want her to be sad. I honestly had that idealistic vision they'd be together forever.

As a human being, I really hate upsetting someone else and if it happens, even unintentionally, I find it very hard to cope and it can trigger a shutdown. The things I reflect upon are hard to admit. I feel that I care about others extremely deeply, yet often my caring is misinterpreted or wrongly perceived, and instead I can come across as cold or unfeeling - which is never my intention. There are three reasons why it might appear this way to someone else:

1. Sometimes I become **so, so involved/concerned for someone else, that I become overwhelmed with emotion.** This is sort of counterproductive because often I just need to retreat to my own space - even if they need me! If I begin to get involved, then it can so quickly become a hurricane of existential trauma and despair. Some people just seem to follow their scripts - a bad event happens, they feel terrible for a time, but they do as they are supposed to and get on with things. It is extremely hard for me to follow this script because bad things weigh heavily in my heart for a long, long time. NTs seem to 'go with the flow' but for me, I have no script and I am thrown off course.

2. **I am quite straight talking and blunt at times, which can make me seem intolerant of others.** I don't mean to come across as rude or

unfeeling, but a part of my character is to be honest and genuine. I just say it as it is.

3. **It is hard for me to feel bad for someone** or feel bad about something that has happened if I have not directly experienced it myself. I think this has something to do with restricted social imagination.

I have strong feelings of being hurt. Minor comments that other people don't give a second thought to, have the ability to ruin an entire day. I remember things for ever. All the comments about being quiet and "weird" at school, I've never forgotten them. I read somewhere that, if someone tells you ninety nine positive things and one negative thing about yourself, you only think about the negative.

Everyone "reacts" to situations; I believe that I am over reactive to situations, where I should just be reactive. My parents describe me as a very "black and white" person. I am "all or nothing." When my weightlifting isn't going as well as it should be, I tend to stop exercising completely. I can feel so discouraged by what I can't do that I won't do anything at all. When I was little, I had temper tantrums and rages really easily; any minor thing could set me off.

I find CBT (Cognitive Behavioural Therapy) very useful. It's helped me to understand that feelings can't actually hurt you and that they do go away. Just because I might feel broken, it doesn't mean I actually am. Intellectually, I understand this concept and I'm trying really hard to use it. People with Asperger's Syndrome often do understand helpful concepts and principles, we just tend to find it more difficult to apply them than people not on the spectrum.

Connecting with others

Although I do not easily connect with other people, I frequently experience a sort of... "sensing" of other people's feelings. On his website, Tony Attwood has talked about how females with Asperger's Syndrome can often be exceptionally sensitive to other people's feelings, particularly the negative ones. I can really relate to this. I wonder if it is because I have had to cope with so much pain, confusion and misunderstanding, that I am able to sense people who are going through a similar experience. Yet I find it much more difficult to imagine, for example, how a child who lost their parents in the 9/11 bombings, is feeling - because I have not experienced the same. I can intellectually comprehend how they might be feeling, but it is much harder for me to actually feel the same way.

In the past, particularly when I was younger, people were not intuitively drawn to me as they were to other people. For example, on my first day at Drama School, I was completely ignored - by both teachers and students. On the first day of secondary school, the other girls seemed to be attracted to one another like magnets. From that day I experienced intense feelings of rejection and awkwardness. Although I still think about this, I am nowhere near as hurt as I once was. Now that I know I have Asperger's Syndrome, I just accept that a lot of the time I don't give off that welcoming, warm vibe that other people do - and it's okay, because I have knowledge about Asperger's Syndrome. Without a diagnosis, I would still be feeling those intense feelings of confusion and hurt. I am happy not talking to people (I always was), but only because now I am old enough to realise it's okay to have my own path, and not follow the crowd. I am still loved. I am me.

Gifts

A large proportion of people on the autistic spectrum have special talents and gifts. There are some things that I'm really good at. From a young age, I was good at writing. When I was 12, I spent a lot of time designing websites and by the time I was 14 I was building computers and competent at web languages.

I love learning and continued my education in science to postgraduate level. Outside of academia, I have strong interests in veterinary medicine, physiology, biomechanics, biochemistry and neuroscience; I don't have qualifications in these subjects but I do find them really interesting and study them in my own time.

When I was 19 I wrote and later published a novel called 'One Lonely Mind[12]' (this is interesting - the main character has Asperger's, though I didn't realise at the time and it wasn't a deliberate character trait). I love books, writing, lifting weights and a few other things. I love cats

12 Rowe, A (2009). One Lonely Mind. London: Lonely Mind Books.

and know all the breeds. I am absorbed in my interests and realise that I need to fit them into my world every day. They are innate loves of mine and I feel uplifted when I engage in them. I wonder whether having such intense special interests has any relationship to being depressed? When I'm unable to pursue my interests, it feels as though my world has been destroyed. I am reliant on these things to get me through each day.

Obsessive interests

People with Asperger's Syndrome tend to have quite specific or obsessive interests. My particular one is my weightlifting. If I could describe how I feel about weightlifting I'd say it's what I live for!

> In many ways, my hobbies are more important than anything else in my life. This is quite common for people with AS. Often, our hobbies will take preference over relationships with other people. It really helps if an NT partner can understand this, otherwise they might feel hurt. It is not personal, but it might appear that way!

I'm so obsessed with weightlifting that I can't ever miss a day's training. When I went to Disneyland Paris, I made sure that our hotel had a gym so that I could do exercise every day and not fall behind on my weightlifting schedule.

> It's a bit ironic that although I dislike travelling and going to places outside of a 3 mile radius around my home, I love Disneyland Paris. Perhaps it's because I love fantasy that I can relax and let go of some of my anxieties about crowds of people and new places.

I think my obsessive interests show dedication and focus, but I admit that my obsessions can sometimes impinge on the "normal" things, such as getting a job and going to work. My interests are so important to me that, when doing them, I lose all sense of everything and zone off into a world where it is just me and nothing else matters. I could talk about weightlifting for hours... and often do!

Here is an example overleaf:

CONVERSATIONS

Sometimes I have a conversation with people, which goes like this:

"Hi Alis. Would you like to meet up tomorrow morning? It's the only time I'm free for a few weeks," says Sam.

"I'm not free tomorrow morning," I reply. "Let's meet in a few weeks when you're free."

"That's a shame. What are you doing in the morning?"

"Weightlifting."

"Oh? Well can't you do it another day instead? Or later on in the day?"

"No."

The only way I can describe it is... my life just doesn't work like that!

People with Asperger's Syndrome appear to function very differently from other people. In this scenario, I was different to Sam, who assumed I was as comfortable and able to accommodate change as she was. The thing is, I'm really particular about routine. I was really looking forward to spending that time on my weightlifting, which is what I find most enjoyable. Whenever someone tries to change my exciting plans I'll feel upset because it feels I've been thrown into a new situation without any chance for preparation.

I need to plan and organise everything. I can't just spontaneously do something, my brain doesn't function in that manner. Even if I was doing nothing one day, had Sam called me on the off chance I might meet her, I'd be unable to do so, through lack of time to prepare. Every time I have to socialise, I have to psyche myself up. The preparation can be physically checking train timetables or researching the intended meeting place, but mostly it involves mentally "energising" myself for the effort it's going to take to be social.

I feel really lost when things change, particularly if something gets in the way of my special interests. Many people not on the autistic spectrum can cope with change much more easily, so they don't understand... or they underestimate what it's like for "someone like me," for whom unexpected change can cause enormous stress.

If you are an NT, it's extremely important to know that you should never take special interests away from us. These interests are what keep us going! If they are taken away from us, it can cause total mental and emotional destruction. Certainly many people have "hobbies," but the big difference between the AS and NT in terms of hobbies is that the AS can be obsessive about them.

A few weeks ago, I fell into a big shutdown because, in a split second, I was unable to do my weightlifting. This is what happened on the next page:

WHEN WEIGHTLIFTING WAS TAKEN AWAY FROM ME

For the last 6 years I've been lifting weights in my garage. I tend to do it in the mornings at 7.30, which I feel is not unreasonably early. One Sunday morning I was in the middle of doing weightlifting when all of a sudden there was a big knock on the garage door. A bit annoyed that my lift was interrupted, I went outside to see who it was. It was our next-door neighbour.

"Look, I'm really sorry but can you please stop the weightlifting? The vibrations are really worrying. We're worried that the books will fall off the shelves. My husband works long hours and he's tired, it wakes us up," she said.

I didn't really know what to say, so I just apologised. After all, I'd been doing it for 6 years so I wondered why it had just become a problem now?

"It's been going on for years but we really tried not to say anything," she carried on speaking, as if she'd read my mind.

At this point I was feeling very angry that she hadn't said anything to me earlier on and had just let this unruly noise carry on. I was also very upset to hear I'd been upsetting someone for such a long time.

"Can you join a gym or something?" she asked.

I felt like shouting "NO!" and then explaining the reasons why I could not join a gym: a) I have AS and it's hard for me to change routine b) you've given me no warning about this c) I've spent lots of money building my own private gym d) I do not like to use other people's equipment when I have expensive, tailored equipment for myself e) it would be hard for me to travel to a public gym every day f) the weightlifting I do is very specific (Olympic lifting) and there aren't any gyms realistically close enough to my house that allow this kind of lifting.
continued...

I asked her if it would be okay to carry on lifting weights if I changed my exercise times from 7.30am to 1.00pm. I thought it was a compromise because at least her husband wouldn't be sleeping.

"We'd rather you didn't. We're worried about the shelves," she said.

So I said "okay" and after that, I ran upstairs to my bedroom and cried.

I realise that she probably felt they'd been putting up with the noise and vibrations for a long time. She probably felt they'd been very accommodating. I am thankful they put up with it, but I wish they would've told me beforehand how noisy it was. I don't like upsetting people and, had I known sooner, I would have had the time to find a solution.

I would have been comfortable meeting her requests but I don't take kindly to change that is so sudden. I needed some warning so that I could prepare/ work out what I was going to do.

This is a brilliant example of the differences between people who are on the spectrum and people who aren't. My neighbour was just totally unaware that she had ruined **my whole world** in the space of a few minutes. This event was the start of another bout of depression.

People with Asperger's Syndrome have strong interests; sometimes it's described as being 'hyperfocused' and is just a part of being on the autistic spectrum. My interests are the "sanctums" I go to when I need to rebuild. If they are disrupted it can cause stress, anxiety and depression. The harder I am finding life the more I need my interests. And in this situation, paradoxically, I really needed my weightlifting even more because I was feeling just so destroyed, and yet the time I needed it most, I was unable to have it.

The days I can't do weightlifting (rest days from the gym or the days I am ill), are extremely long and tedious. Suddenly my existence feels like a huge void. Whereas other people might be able to fill this void seeing their friends or socialising, I cannot do this - and I would rather be my myself than with others, even if I am bored.

Sharing favourite things

The majority of the time I am comfortable sharing things with other people. For example, I'll happily lend someone a book. However, there are boundaries, and when it comes to certain things it's extremely hard for me to share them with other people.

As an example, I am very possessive about my weightlifting space and equipment. Over a number of years our family has built up an excellent gym in our house. I don't mind them using the cardio machines, but my sister occasionally has phases where she wants to lift weights. I get unbelievably distraught about this and, to be honest, the real reason is that weightlifting is my hobby and I don't want to share my gym with anyone else.

> To be honest, I don't know why I am so reactive to my sister using my weightlifting equipment. It just really upsets me. I don't like people encroaching on my territory, even if they're family. I don't even like training with someone else as I need to be absorbed in my own routine and agenda.

Rigidity and inflexibility

People with AS are known to be quite rigid. Personally I love planning and planning in advance is important to me. Sticking to time accurately is also essential for me to live as secure a life as possible. I feel anxious if things are not on time. I remember how much it used to distress me when teachers were 5 minutes late to start the lesson at school, or when the same boy was late for class every time. It makes me very upset and frustrated when the train is delayed.

I have to be punctual for everything and even being five minutes late can completely disrupt my schedule and cause me to feel very upset and anxious.

Here is an example of something that once happened to me:

PARTICIPATION IN AUTISM RESEARCH IN LONDON

I had volunteered to be a participant for some autism research in London. The research start time was 9.00am, but the letter told us to arrive at 8:50am. The night before I planned my journey very carefully to ensure I would arrive at 8:50am or before, so that I wouldn't be late. As expected, I arrived at the venue with time to spare and waited for the other participants to join me.

At 8:50am, four of us out of the total five were present but the fifth person was yet to show up. The researcher phoned the person to check she was on her way. When she'd finished the phone call, she relayed to the rest of us that participant number five was "just a bit lost," and consequently the researcher decided that we should all wait for a few more minutes in the hope that she would join us soon.

Now, this distressed me because a) I felt that myself and the other four people had all made a big effort to arrive at the correct time so what had been the point, if we'd all had to end up waiting anyway? b) my whole day was now delayed because, if we started late, we were going to end the day late too - which would mean I'd have to take a later train back home, eat lunch at a later time than usual, and have a late gym workout.

I felt like I was being "punished." I don't know if that makes sense to you. It does to me. I blamed the researcher, even though this may be seen as unreasonable.

You might notice it was impossible for me to see the other person's point of view (perhaps she hadn't felt well that morning and was running late), as I was overwhelmed with my own stress. The researcher knew that everyone had an autistic disorder so she should have managed the situation differently. The other group members were probably feeling just as distressed.

I routinely question whether people ever actually think about the impact their actions have on other people and the consequences for them... On the other hand, it is hard for me to think of the impact I have on them!

This man bends down to tie up his shoelace in the very middle of the pavement. The other pedestrians have to manoeuvre past him. I think it is inconsiderate of him. He isn't thinking about how his actions are affecting everyone around him. (My mum however says I do this without thinking! I don't think I do).

Attention to detail

One of my favourite attributes is my attention to detail. This shows itself most when I listen to or read books.

In my head I have an image and a vision of how written words should be presented. If the words don't match what I feel they should, I get extremely distracted and distressed. I am unable to continue reading because all I am thinking about is how I would change the words. I don't know exactly why I am like this, but I have a close eye for incorrectly spelt words or incorrect punctuation. When I look at something, the first thing I notice will be that missing apostrophe or spelling mistake.

As an example, there's a local hairdresser's shop and on its sign it says "Maries hair cutting." I'm sure most people would simply 'get the message' that Marie is the lady who does hair cutting, but all I can focus on is the missing apostrophe after the "e" in her name. In my mind I have a vivid picture of somebody who is careless and I feel they should know better. From my point of view, they are not giving the correct impression.

When I was doing my A levels I had a biology teacher whose written language was appalling. He spoke and read English fluently, but he just couldn't write. I had so much trouble concentrating in those classes; all I'd see were the spelling mistakes or missing commas, I'd totally miss the point of the slide. I was just fixated on the writing! I don't think the other students even noticed his mistakes. Needless to say, I didn't learn a lot in those lessons.

I didn't have sympathy for him. In hindsight, he could've been dyslexic, or English could've been his second language. Maybe he was trying really hard. I guess, to me, he was the teacher and should've been setting an example. I was strongly recognising his role as a teacher and didn't think he was fulfilling it. I wanted to tell him but I knew not to.

I also get extremely confused if I'm reading something and the wrong word has been used (for example, "complementary" instead of "complimentary"). I wonder whether a lot of people would even notice? But I am unable to continue reading; I get so totally lost in my flow that I have to go back and re-read the sentence multiple times. I just get so bewildered and flustered. On the other hand, my own use of language is quite unusual and can be hard to follow. But my apostrophes will always be correct!

Taking things literally

I've always been an avid reader and I did really well at English in school. I know about metaphors and am quick to recognise them in books. But although I understand non-literal phrases, it takes me a bit longer to process them than perhaps it does for other people. I've "learned" to realise when people are speaking literally and when they are not, however because it takes me a longer time to process these types of phrases, I often feel flustered.

One of my earliest memories of being a bit confused about literal language was when I was about 18 and it was quite trendy to be "going out for coffee" with your friends. The first time I heard this, I was quite worried because I hate coffee. Several coffee shop meetings later, I realised that "going out for coffee" didn't necessarily mean that; it could mean other drinks that I liked, such as tea or hot chocolate. It does confuse me though, that society has chosen to use "coffee" to mean not only coffee but also any other drink you like! It's the same when people say they are "going out for drinks," which apparently means alcoholic drinks. I was always so confused as a teenager when people asked me, "do you drink?" because I did not instinctively realise they were referring to alcohol. Of course I drink, otherwise I wouldn't be alive!

To me, all these phrases are just inaccurate. So my personal preference is to always be straightforward with people and I'll say things like "I'm going to the cafe to have a cup of tea. Would you like to come?" or "I don't drink alcohol" rather than just "I don't drink," a phrase which seems unbelievably silly to me!

My mum once asked me to go and buy a bag that she'd had her eye on from a shop, because she was too busy to go herself. It was an interesting scenario:

GIFT WRAPPING

At the counter, the shop assistant asked me if the bag was a gift. I said yes, because it wasn't for me, it was for my mum and in my mind, buying something for someone else constitutes as a gift. Immediately the assistant started wrapping the bag in gift paper. There was a delayed reaction from me while I processed what she'd meant and then I started feeling very flustered because I realised I should have said no, not yes. I did not want the bag to be gift wrapped. As an AS, I wish people would be more clear in what they say. She had not explicitly asked me if I wanted the bag to be gift wrapped.

It took several minutes to wrap the bag so I had enough time to process the situation and calm my flustered feelings. When she asked me if I wanted a gift receipt, I knew the correct answer was no. I had no idea what this was, so I just told her that I wanted a normal receipt.

I'd never experienced this simple situation before, which is why I got confused. I need to add the gift wrapping question to my 'book of common phrases by NTs and what they really mean.' People with AS would find life a lot easier if they took the time to learn about these day to day experiences and expressions.

Reading faces

People on the autistic spectrum have problems with communication and one of the ways humans communicate is through our facial expressions. I'm better now that I'm older, but when I was little I was always asking my mum if she was cross, when there was nothing wrong at all.

One of the reasons I like animated cartoons and movies is that their expressions and body language are exaggerated to such an extent it feels like there's less "going on" in comparison to when there's a real person in a film. In cartoons, the non-verbal messages are obvious. I am able to follow a character's speaking and physical mannerisms or expressions at the same time. I wonder whether this is why my two of my favourite hobbies are reading and listening to audio stories? Both of them are emotional tasks which I can concentrate on with just one sensory medium at a time. I can use my eyes to read the words in a book or my ears to listen to the voice on the CD. Otherwise I can easily feel overloaded.

My own use of language can be rather formal or may be muddled. I have very limited emotional vocabulary. I can usually only explain that I am feeling either sad or happy. This can be confusing for everyone, including me.

Perfectionism

I've read that having perfectionist tendencies makes you more likely to be a sufferer of depression. I've suffered from a somewhat "neurotic" perfectionism; in the past I've not been able to be happy with anything less than one hundred percent and I'll dwell on mistakes.

I remember when I was 17 and received a B grade for one of my exams (I was expecting an A). I was so disappointed and I dwelled on the result for many days afterwards.

> Be kind to yourself! Aspies often have high standards. This means we set ourselves up for many failures, which can make us feel extremely sad and disappointed.

I can happily say that getting older has helped me and, although I'm still a perfectionist, my perfectionism is now a lot more controlled! It's taken some time (as well as some disappointing results) but I'm now more understanding, given my greater degree of self awareness.

Recently I had an exam and, unfortunately on that day I was having a big emotional episode; I hadn't slept well and was curled up in bed crying my eyes out that morning. There were three hours left before the exam. After some words of encouragement and some "pushing" from my parents (see later), I decided to take the exam. I got a high grade, but not the highest.

In the past I would've been disappointed about not having achieved the highest grade, but on that day I was really happy. I accepted that I hadn't felt well that day and I congratulated myself for taking the exam, regardless of how unwell I'd been feeling.

I've done some public speaking in the past (something I hate and certainly doesn't come naturally to me). My talks will never be amazing, but I've come to accept this. I'm not particularly charismatic and I'm shy; but I know that I am very good at some things, and less good at others.

I imagine in the future if I was in employment, I'd talk to my manager about my skills and my limitations. I'd make it clear that it was not best use of my time to deliver presentations, but I'd be okay at creating them. I'd explain for example, I'm not the best speaker on the phone, but I'm really professional at email communication.

If you're struggling at work, consider speaking with your boss about the things you are good at and the things you find hard. You might be pleasantly surprised to find the things you are good at are the things that other people find excruciatingly boring. That means more nice work for you!

As somebody with AS, it's very important to find things you are good at and enjoy and ensure you pursue them. I'm really glad I've found weightlifting and I'm very good at it. By doing it every day it makes me feel a lot happier and more confident. I get to indulge true to my perfectionistic tendencies in the things that really matter to me, such as my weightlifting and my writing. In the past, I would try to be perfect at everything, but no one is perfect at everything and I've come to accept that.

People on the autistic spectrum usually feel "different" and "misplaced," so it's vital we're able to find our special place in the world in the form of a hobby or project. We can fulfil our natural perfectionistic tendencies in something we are good at!

Asperger's Syndrome 'Shutdowns' and 'Meltdowns'

People on the autistic spectrum tend to have extreme reactions to stimuli. These are known as either 'shutdowns' or 'meltdowns.' There are usually two ways in which we can react. Depending on one's particular personality, some may be more prone to one or the other. In my experience, meltdowns and shutdowns generally compare like this:

	Shutdowns	Meltdowns
Presentation	A fierce rage against a situation	A retreat
Personality type more likely to be affected	More independent or sure of themselves; perhaps more extroverted	More passive; perhaps more introverted
Response	Anger, screaming, outbursts, aggression, crying	Total exhaustion; total 'close off' from the world
The best way to respond	Leave them alone in a quiet room to calm down on their own	Approach and talk to them quietly and soothingly

Please note, meltdowns and shutdowns don't always mean we are depressed, although they may be components of depression and our way of coping. Some people drink alcohol as a coping mechanism... we tend to either melt down or shut down.

When I was little, I had more meltdowns than shutdowns. I was a really hyperactive child who had temper tantrums and got angry or upset very easily. By the time I reached adolescence, I definitely had more shutdowns and now, as an adult, I have shutdowns exclusively. It's interesting how my behaviour has changed over time.

Have a look at this graph:

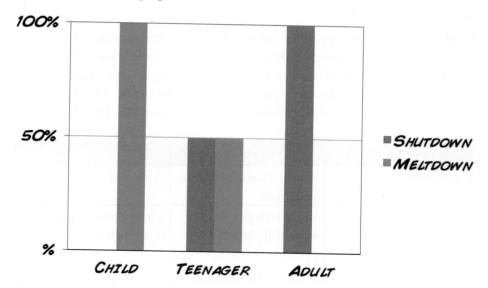

There's a lot less information about shutdowns than meltdowns, maybe because they can be tricky to explain. The best explanation I've found is this one:

'Imagine buying a brand new computer that works, is state of the art and in top condition. Imagine a continued usage of that computer without turning it off once. Regardless of the computer's quality, it will always become overheated and will need to be switched off at some point in order for it to work perfectly again.' (Bryan Chandler[13], 2013)

Now imagine you are the computer that wakes up in a really good mood and in top condition. Imagine "using" yourself continually for social activities and events without once taking a break. Regardless of how happy your mood may be, it will always become difficult on occasions and you will need to switch off in order for you to work perfectly again.

13 Bryan Chandler. (2013). In Facebook [Community page]. Retrieved February, 21, 2013, from http://www.facebook.com/AspergerSyndromeAwareness

An AS in shutdown may appear cold, distant or insensitive, but honestly this isn't the case - we're just trying to recuperate from a situation that has been stressful for us. Don't feel offended.

My own shutdowns can be caused by anything. It could be a result of something someone has said, watching something distressing on T.V., a disruption in my routine, or a combination of things.

The worst shutdowns are the ones that are built up from lots of different things. It doesn't matter how small or big the scenario is to someone else. It could be anything from as terrible as someone's death or as simple as a joke I took the wrong way, the event will have the same consequence: shutdown.

Aspies are hypersensitive. This means our brains get overloaded quickly. Shutdowns or meltdowns often occur because we've been exposed to too many things or too many people, ultimately causing sensory overload.

Shutdowns can come on either gradually, over a few days or even weeks, or they can come on in an instant.

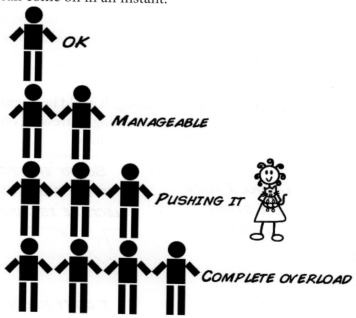

OK

MANAGEABLE

PUSHING IT

COMPLETE OVERLOAD

The more people or things I am exposed to, the more stressful the situation becomes.

You may notice that my reactions do not necessarily correlate with the significance of the event, in contrast to most neurotypical people.

What happens to me during my shutdowns?

Honestly, life has just got too much and I zone out into my own world. I usually go to my bedroom and curl up in bed, pull the blankets very close around me because I feel safe surrounded by blankets pressing down on me. I like to put my hands or pillows over my ears because they get very hot and tight when I feel overwhelmed. When I am shut down I like to be left alone in my dark bedroom. The best way to get me out of it is when my mum comes upstairs, speaks quietly and soothingly and gives me a hug. I do not want to have anyone else around me though, just my mum.

The best way I can describe feeling shut down is like it's going into "hibernation" for a period of time. Some episodes last several days, and I won't speak to anybody or I'm unlikely to leave the house. I also like to switch my phone off for several days.

When we go into shutdown mode, we aren't always in a bad mood. We experience a lot of overwhelming senses on a daily basis. When we are in shutdown, it's getting rid of the stress of those senses and achieving "comfortable blankness." It is a restorative procedure... a sensory timeout. Not a bad mood.

Shutdowns or Depression?

I used to say I was "sad" when I was experiencing a shutdown. Then I said "depressed." Now I realise that shutdowns and clinical depression are not quite the same. But shutdown can turn into depression.

	My shutdowns	My clinical depression
Length	Days	Weeks to months
Mood	Zoned out	Sad, empty, numb
Appetite	OK	Increases or decreases
Sleep	OK	Broken, early wakening
Energy	Exhausted	Exhausted
Pleasure in hobbies	Want to lift weights but can't	Don't enjoy anything
Suicidal feelings	None	Intense
Feeling guilty or a burden to others	A bit, as I am in shutdown	High
Anxiety	No	High
Concentration	Poor	Poor
How I describe my feelings to others	"Sad"	"Sad"

Being hypermobile

I was always really flexible as a child. My parents said I used to bend in all kind of weird directions. I could spontaneously collapse on the floor safely and relaxed. I've never broken a bone and I can't imagine I ever would - my body just feels like it could simply adjust itself to prevent any kind of injury. Maybe that's why I feel affinity with cats!

One of the best things a person with joint hypermobility can do is build strength, so it's funny (and beneficial!) that I just happened to get into weightlifting! I've been diagnosed with Joint Hypermobility Syndrome, so since my ligaments can't support my bones, my muscles need to do all the work. It's fortunate that I've been lifting weights for 6 years then. Hypermobility can also lead to poor posture, which I have. Even though I do lots of stretching and rehabilitation, I have a tendency to hunch up.

When I first learned about Asperger's Syndrome, it was really interesting to discover that lots of us are hypermobile.

Some people with Asperger's Syndrome are thin or skinny with underdeveloped muscle. It might be helpful to consider taking up exercise, such as yoga, pilates, cycling or weightlifting. Your body will feel stronger, you'll probably have less aches and pains and you might feel better about your appearance. Exercise improves sleep quality too, which is never a bad thing for an Aspie! Many of us suffer from insomnia.

Aching muscles

It might be the combination of being physically active and being autistic, but most of the time, I have achy muscles. When you are a weightlifter, some muscle pain is expected, but I still have intense memories of aching muscles a long time before I started lifting weights.

When I was going through puberty I had the most agonising muscle and joint pains, which we put down to growth spurts (it probably was, but I think sensitivity due to autism also played its part). Somewhere I read that a few people on the autistic spectrum experience muscle cramps or aches. I feel as if all my stress embeds itself in my muscles. Even though I don't like touch, **I love, love, love deep massage**. It gets rid of all my aches, pains, stresses, and anxieties. When I was little, my dad used to rub pain relieving gel on to my legs before I went to bed. Sometimes in the night I'd wake up with excruciating muscle pain and my parents would have to come in to my room and massage my legs, to send me back to sleep.

When your AS daughter, son or partner feels stressed, offer to massage them. Brushing their hair may be extremely uncomfortable for them but firm massage can be extremely stress-relieving. There are also self-massaging devices you can buy. One of my favourite things is my hockey ball. I lie on it on the floor and rub my muscles over it. It's very hard. You can also use a tennis ball.

Coordination and clumsiness

Many people with Asperger's Syndrome have problems with their motor coordination. Some people are clumsy but I've mostly noticed that I have problems learning new movements. Many people call this dyspraxia.

At school, sometimes we did dancing but no matter how hard I tried, I could never do it. Certainly I was shy which didn't help, but there was always a kind of "block" around me which meant I was simply unable to process rhythm, sound and movement all at the same time. I can't remember dance steps at the same time as trying to do them. Once, at a work party, I was pressurised into going on a dance machine and everyone laughed at just how bad I was, even though I tried so hard. My friend and I had tennis coaching every week for about a year but despite everything, by the end of the year I still could not hit the ball correctly!

Looking back on dancing at school, I wonder whether dancing has just too many sensory inputs, such as music, lights, reflections, bright flooring and other dancers. These, in combination with being shy and having poor rhythm, made dancing impossible.

It's funny though, despite being unable to hit a tennis ball with a racket and being totally unable to dance, I am very good at Olympic weightlifting. It's my favourite thing but I mustn't go on about it too much....! Olympic weightlifting involves very technical, difficult and complicated movements that take many years to master, but I did not seem to have any problems learning them. The movements just feel very natural and comfortable when I do them. I think that, because I train alone, there's no pressure to keep up with anybody else - weightlifting is a very solitary sport and maybe having less environmental stimuli (it's just me and the bar, no music, lights or even mirrors etc.), means I can fully focus. Weightlifting is learned gradually over time and I've learned to know what to feel and look for in the movements. I have learned patience and, in return, I am able to replicate the movements that Olympic weightlifters do.

> Weightlifting gives me peace and tranquillity. All I have is a solid, zinc bar and some weight plates. There is no music and no lights. No other people. It's very private and therapeutic. Weightlifting gives me my rebuilding time.

Team sports require cooperation but that just goes over my head. It takes a lot of coordination to think about what the opponent is doing as well as cooperating with team members.

> People with AS may be better suited to more solitary sports, such as weightlifting, yoga, pilates or cycling. Bear in mind that cycling, which requires coordination and motor skills, might take longer to master so requires patience. Swimming is a good sport but is often bright and noisy. In the Olympic stadium at London 2012, there was complete silence when weights were being lifted.

I also enjoy cycling, but I had trouble learning when I was little and it took me longer to learn than most other children. I believe that the only reason I passed the 'Cycling Proficiency' scheme was because I replicated exactly the motions the girl before me was doing. I did not understand and could not follow the instructions spoken by the instructor.

It still takes me a long time to process left and right. Even though I've known the difference for years and years, it takes me several seconds to actually feel confident I have them the right way round.

Diet

Many children with Asperger's Syndrome, particularly boys, are put off by food because of either its colour or its texture. I love eating and indeed one of my favourite things about food is the range of textures and how they feel in my mouth. When I had an operation to my jaw (because my upper and lower teeth did not meet; I had no 'bite'), I was consuming a liquid diet for a number of weeks. This was excruciatingly hard for someone who loves to eat! Interestingly, what I missed most of all was actually the texture of food, rather than its taste. I love food that I can crunch, melt, chew, suck or gnaw; all the different ways feel amazing. I am a weightlifter (have I told you that yet?) so eating a healthy, balanced diet is crucial to fuel my training. I'm also aware that when I eat badly, I feel bad too. My diet definitely has an impact on my mood. Even though I eat the same things every day, I do make sure I get all the 'food groups' in the right proportions and I am careful to get all the vitamins and minerals I need. I never miss meals, I eat regularly at the same times, and always eat breakfast. Eating this way gives me the energy I need to get through each day. I feel I need more energy than most people, because my brain is continuously processing all this incoming data from the world around me. But maybe it's just the weightlifting (how did I manage to get back to that...).

A balanced diet is important for anyone! But since people with Asperger's Syndrome are more prone to mood swings, good nutrition can help keep the brain functioning properly. It could be said we have to work extra hard 24/7 to make sense of a very complicated world!

My current daily diet is 3 eggs on 4 pieces of wholemeal toast in the morning, a bowl of tuna, sweetcorn and mayonnaise at lunch, tins of peas and carrots as snacks, and 3 eggs on 4 pieces of wholemeal toast for dinner. Twice a week I will have rainbow trout instead of tuna for lunch.

I'll probably eat this diet religiously for about six months, until I finally get bored. It's only when I get that "overdose" feeling from eating the same thing for so long that I decide to change my diet - but never until I get that feeling. My eating phases are cycles that last anywhere from six months to a year and in that time period I won't vary my diet at all.

For the past six months I have been eating tins of peas and carrots, non-stop. I still eat my other things, but I have to have those every day too. Before that it was beetroot for lunch, dinner and snacks. I have been obsessed with margherita pizza and will *only* ever eat at restaurants that serve them. I even have a blog which reviews margherita pizzas from all different restaurants.

I have trouble understanding people who like eating different things throughout the week. I've never experienced the dilemmas I hear routinely in my house, in public or with friends, such as:

It would feel very strange for me if I had to eat different things all the time. I've been out to dinner and the other guests can take forever to decide what they're going to eat, whereas I already know and will have already chosen. When I find something I like to eat, put simply, **I just like it**... and don't crave anything else. It takes me months to get bored of something, even if I eat it multiple times a day. It does not appeal to me to eat different foods all the time. My diet is very much, 'if it's not broken, don't fix it.' I also do not understand the reluctance of some people to eat certain foods only at appropriate times, for example scrambled eggs on toast should only be eaten at breakfast. I have gone through an entire year eating one particular type of cottage pie for breakfast.

I do not like it when people call me a fussy eater or ask me why I'm not eating anything at the time. I have a sensible, rigid eating routine and I'll always know what I plan on eating and when. I do not like it when people try and give me food when either I've already eaten or I'll be eating shortly. I hope I don't show my annoyance but, if I do, it's because my routine is being tampered with! I prefer to eat at home, where I can have some quiet time.

People with Asperger's Syndrome have habits and routines! If we like our routines, don't try and change them... If you ask someone with AS to "try this" and they say "no," please accept that they really mean no!

I have a sort of "phobia" of fruit. It is the one dominant thing I do not like and do not like others to be eating it around me. The smell of fruit, particularly oranges and bananas, is overpowering and makes me feel physically sick. I do not like the look of fruit either. I love biscuits and cake but I cannot eat any which have been stored near or have touched a piece of fruit. If someone has just eaten a banana and then offers me a slice of cake, I will say no... even though I want the cake, unless they've washed their hands I'm unable to eat it. When I was younger, I always asked anyone in my family who had eaten fruit to go and brush their teeth!

We often have heightened sensory perceptions which means certain smells can be extremely overpowering and can cause us to feel sick.

Like many people on the autism spectrum, I go through food "obsessions." These have included cottage pie, beetroot, and soya beans.

You might find this story funny:

LOW THYROXINE AND SOYA BEANS

I went through a phase of eating two huge packs of soya beans every single day for months. During this period I started to feel unwell, with symptoms of tiredness, blurred vision, and fainting. I went to the doctor and had a blood test and the results showed I had low thyroid levels. When I went home I started to research foods to help improve metabolism and thyroid function and discovered that too much soya can actually be bad for your thyroid. I told the doctor I'd been eating "lots of soya" but she sort of just shrugged it off, and I wonder if she had any idea just how much "lots" actually meant to someone with Asperger's Syndrome! When I get obsessed about something, I'll pursue it relentlessly.

The good news is, when I reduced the quantity of soya beans I was eating, my thyroid levels went back to normal very quickly! This was a very easy and simple solution!

We have our groceries home delivered every week and my parents always joke with me about what the pickers must think when they get our order ready. I choose very specific things, in large quantities - because I only eat a small range of foods. For example I will order 25 tins of peas for the week. I am also particular about brands - things must always be the same brand and I send back any items that get substituted. I wonder if other people have orders that are similar to mine?

I get extremely distressed if I go into the supermarket to buy a certain item, only to find it's out of stock. I'm sure most people would simply pick up an alternative, problem solved. However, this disruption causes total emotional chaos for me. I have not planned for this to happen and suddenly I feel very lost and confused. I just stand there not knowing what to do, because now my whole dinner routine has changed...

When we went to Disneyland Paris, I brought my own food in Tupperware and cooler bags just in case there wasn't going to be anything I wanted to eat. I'm really glad I did, because it turned out the food available in the park unsurprisingly did not suit me. I really missed my vegetables whilst we were there, so we went in search of a supermarket and stocked up on tins of French vegetables to take back to our hotel. Here's another funny story:

THE TINNED VEG AND AIRPORT STORY

The French vegetables were so delicious that I wanted to buy some to take home with me. I bought lots of them and packed them into my suitcase. At the French airport, I was stopped at the security gate because they'd detected metal in my bag! In front of everyone, the guards opened up my suitcase... only to find 30 cans of vegetables. They looked at one another in bemusement, before saying, "...Yeah, everything's okay, it's just... veg!" I wonder how many other people they've had to stop because they'd brought tinned vegetables home.

Hypersensitivity

When I am with other people, I realise that they usually take a lot of things for granted and do not think much about the small things going on around them. My concentration and thoughts get hijacked because I see discrepancy and disorder in everything, that most people seem unaware of. I often consider myself an observer of life, rather than a participant, and I take pleasure in studying the world around me.

> People with AS often feel like observers. Many feel they are here to simply study the world but never be a part of it.

For me, life offers a completely new sensation every day. For example, someone may eat a sandwich and not really notice how it tastes because they think they already know. But for me, that same sandwich will taste incredible every time.

I am really sensitive to everything. Sometimes this can be a good thing, because I am more aware of things such as traffic on the road. I can probably also tell you that your phone has just vibrated when you couldn't hear it. On the other hand, being really sensitive can be very, very distracting and stressful. My senses of smell and sound can make everyday noises and smells hard to tolerate, and I am very sensitive to touch.

Imagine if you are in a busy coffee bar trying to have a conversation with a friend. People are rushing in and out with their coffees-to-go. The music is blaring from the speakers in the ceiling. The sun is very brightly shining in through the big glass windows. Someone drops a mug and it makes a huge crashing sound. The couple next to you are having a conversation about their summer holiday plans.

Now, can you imagine trying to have that conversation with your friend?

Of course there are ways of getting through these situations. I carry earplugs and sunglasses with me wherever I go. I try to visit coffee bars during quiet times. But there are always similar situations occurring on a daily basis.

I like wearing noise-dampening ear plugs in public places, such as cafes or the cinema. Some people wear sunshades all the time. Have you tried these potential solutions?

Touch

I remember when my sister used to pluck my eyebrows - it was such a nightmare because I just shook and tensed up whenever she came near me. For some reason, the only way I could tolerate it was to cover my eyes with my hands. In jest, she said she hoped I never have treatment from a beauty therapist because they'd find my response just ridiculous! As a therapist, she'd never come across someone who behaved like me during an eyebrow shaping procedure.

I dislike and shy away from any sort of physical contact with another person. Some examples of contact that I do not like are:

- Hand shake
- Kiss on the cheek
- Brief hug
- Sitting on a seat close to someone else
- Tap on the shoulder

I always feel really uncomfortable. Most people make me "recoil" in terms of physical touch. I know we all have 'personal space,' but I think my personal space must be bigger than the average person's. If I'm on the train I'd much rather stand up for the whole journey rather than sit on the tiny, narrow seats that are so close together that my legs often touch the person beside. I also find it to be 'too close for comfort' if I can feel the warmth of a chair that someone else has just left.

Something that troubles me a bit, is seating plans in cafes. Have you ever come across those cafes that have two comfy armchairs that are arranged like this:

In my mind, this is one bit of personal space, i.e. it is space for a single person. Even though there are two armchairs, they are so close that I feel that if someone is sitting on Seat 1 then someone who isn't with them should not sit on Seat 2. But from my observation of people in the cafe environment, it's socially acceptable for two people who don't know each other to sit on Seats 1 and 2 when it is busy (or sometimes even when it isn't!). Out of choice, I don't feel comfortable on either Seat 1 or Seat 2 when a stranger is on the other seat. It just feels too close! I value my personal space, even in public places. Another example is if you are on the treadmill at the gym and there is a whole row of empty treadmills, yet another person chooses to use the one right next to you. Many neurotypicals will feel a bit the same, it's just **VERY intense** for me, so much so I can be disrupted for the rest of the day.

I like my parents, sister, and Granny to hug me when I am feeling sad, but they are the only people who I will let hug me; and even then there are times where I don't want to be hugged at all, not by them or by anyone. Hugging typically only ever happens if I am the initiator and anyone who knows me well is very careful about when to touch me. I guess I'm like a cat, I like affection but only if I come to you.

 I also have problems tolerating unintentional contact, such as a hand brushing me when I'm next to someone on the settee, or when someone brushes me slightly walking past me in the street. I don't like sleeping close to someone because the feeling of their breath on my skin or the touch of their arm or leg against mine, is so intense it can be unbearable and make me feel stressed. There are times when other people can be touching so lightly I don't think they even realise it, but if this happens to me the sensations are always felt intensely. Imagine that feeling you get when you cut your nails too short. It's uncomfortable for a while but then it goes away. That discomfort for me never goes away. When I am touched, the sensation and perception linger for a long time, even after the initial contact has ended. Just that sensation of sitting next to someone on the train can remain with me for hours after the journey has ended.

When I was a child most of my family members "accepted" that I did not like to be touched. My favourite aunt would always say, "I know you don't like being kissed so I'll blow you one instead." She is lovely.

I love cuddles with animals though! I'm lucky we always had pets growing up. When I was little, my favourite thing to stroke were the velvety ears of our black Cocker Spaniel. We currently have five big, cuddly cats and two kittens that I kiss and hug all the time; and one of them sleeps under my underarm, right up close to me.

The way I look is always decided by comfort. I don't really care what clothes look like, so long as they feel nice. I'll wear clothing I don't like the look of, so long as they are comfortable. I have a limited number of clothes and wear the same outfits on rotation. If I find something I really like I'll buy many items of the same, so that I always have backup if they wear out!

> Parents probably need to spend a lot of effort and time allowing their children to try on all sorts of different clothes, until they find clothing that's comfortable.

I used to be bothered about what people thought of the way I dressed. Now I am more comfortable simply wearing what I want to for whatever activity I am doing. I am fortunate that my lifestyle is more relaxed, but this might not be the case for everyone, for example for those who work in offices. I have found that dying clothing is a useful way to be wearing something different.

> For some reason NTs place a lot of emphasis on having different outfits for different occasions. I don't understand this - to me, clothing is all about feeling comfortable! But apparently these social rules are quite important and we should be able to adjust to some degree. It might be a good idea to introduce your children at an early age to social conventions regarding dress. You could show your children pictures of people wearing different outfits for different things and explain the reasons why they are wearing them.

Sound

I have so many problems with sound that even my own breathing and heartbeat can bother me. Even silence is deafeningly loud and I sleep best when I have the fan on all night (even in the winter). I always wear earplugs when I go to the cinema because movies are really loud and the plugs soften the sounds. I love wearing earplugs when I am anywhere outside my house. They are comfortable and soothing and they make me feel as though I'm living in another dimension.

I listen to audio CD stories every night but it's such a hassle having to adjust the volume up and down all the time. Different narrators have different pitches and volumes - so for one narrator I will have to listen to them at a volume of 18, whereas another might be as high as 29. Even in a single story, the narrator will often change his or her tone or pitch to emphasise certain aspects - such as laughter or shouting. When this happens, I have to turn the volume down. But when they whisper, I need to turn it up. It is very annoying and time-consuming. I wish I could just set the volume to one level, relax and enjoy the whole story, rather than continually pressing the volume buttons up and down.

My dad spends time every evening packing up boxes to be taken to the post office. The sound of the brown packing tape is so sharp it's unbearable. It sounds like nails on a chalk board. I can hear it all the way two floors up to my bedroom, which is in the attic.

> Take note that sounds that are merely loud to you can be completely overwhelming for us. A good example is firework night. To most people, fireworks are fun and exciting but to many with Asperger's Syndrome, they are very distressing.

I've had tinnitus for a while, which may be related to having an autistic spectrum disorder. I have heard this is not uncommon...

Smell

My sense of smell is very, very strong. I often think that if I had a choice to get rid of one sense, it would be smell. I like lots of smells but there are far, far too many smells I don't like. The smells I detest the most are: bananas, all fruit, popcorn, dustbins and general waste, stale washing machines or dishwashers. I have a vivid memory of going to a dinner party when I was about 10 years old. Our friends were lovely and the food was delicious - yet the pleasure of the experience was ruined because the dishwasher was behind my chair and I did not like the smell every time it was opened.

I have really noticed that people seem to love eating bananas. They love to eat them in their houses, in the street and in coffee shops, but the worst place is on the train! Pretty much every time I take the train (which isn't even that often at all), it's guaranteed there will be someone in my carriage who decides to peel a banana! Within milliseconds, I can smell it. I have to move to another carriage because **I just can't stand the smell**, it makes me feel sick.

There is a particular franchised coffee shop that I like to go to. However, what bothers me most, is the communal milk and sugar table. This is where you go to get milk and sugar after you've bought your drink. I do not like this table because not only is it very small, crowded and always messy, but the bin is there too. The bin is an open "hole" in the middle of the table and it is always very strong smelling. Sometimes if I look inside there is a smelly banana skin. I do not think it is very pleasant having a waste container that does not close, especially in a coffee shop where people come to enjoy the aroma of food and drink.

It's really hard when I go out with someone and they order an orange juice (if they know me well enough they really shouldn't be ordering one). If I am not totally at ease with them, it can be awkward to ask them whether they would please mind having another drink instead. Sitting at a table with a glass of orange juice very close to me makes me feel sick.

One time my friend had been drinking something and I could definitely smell fruit. This friend knows I don't like fruit and doesn't usually drink it if he knows he's about to see me. So I asked him if he had been drinking a fruit-flavoured drink, but he said no. I was certain he was either misinformed or fibbing because I just knew my sense of smell would not be wrong. After seeing me, I asked him to go and check the ingredients on the can. When he looked, it contained mixed fruit flavours!

Our household waste and recycling is collected on Fridays. I really dread this day because there are always lots of dustbin lorries driving around and the smell is just disgusting. My mode of transport is either to cycle or walk, so unfortunately I regularly come in close contact with the lorries. I have to take an enormous breath of fresh air before I go past one, and will only breathe out a long distance after I've passed. These smells are very potent and unpleasant but the smell of popcorn is one that actually makes me physically unable to breathe. That smell is suffocating and am unable to go to the cinema and sit near someone who is eating popcorn.

Keeping clean

It's a number one priority for me to wash my hands as soon as I come home from being outside and I appreciate it when other people do the same.

Recently I went to see a physiotherapist. I was in the waiting room and he came out of his room carrying a black waste bag that he was taking outside. When he came back, he invited me into his room and then proceeded with his assessment. I was extremely conscious that he had not washed his hands and that he would imminently be touching my skin. It was all I could think about, but I was too shy to ask him if he'd please mind washing his hands. He'd either just forgotten or it didn't occur to him as something he needed to do. Sometimes I wish I could be like others and just not care, it's such a huge effort being like this.

> Looking back, I think I should have politely said to him something like "I'm a bit OCD about keeping clean. Would you mind washing your hands?" I have noticed that the phrase "I'm a bit OCD" is generally taken well. It seems to be an acceptable social phrase.

I have a great aversion to waste bins and won't touch them. At home, we have one with a swing lid so my hands never have to come in contact. The one in my bedroom has a foot pedal. When I'm out in public, I'd rather hold on to my rubbish until I find a bin that doesn't require me to touch it.

Interestingly though... I'm not that bothered about keeping my own bedroom spotlessly clean. In my mind, I feel since it's only really me who lives in it, it's only my own "dirt" that I'm living with - which I find totally acceptable (there are no banana skins, for example!). I feel the same about bedsheets. I know that you are supposed to change your bedding regularly, but I am oblivious as to knowing when I need to change my own. My bedding always feels comfortable and cosy. It doesn't cross my mind to change it very often. Again, if it's only me who sleeps in my bed then it's only my dirt. I take showers at least every day and wash my hands very frequently. I do not consider I might transfer much dirt or dust to my bed.

7.
Work and University

Jobs

I have trouble finding and keeping jobs, simply because a job has to be appropriate for my personality. I have a lot of social anxiety just leaving my house, let alone being committed to a job for a period of time. In most jobs I've had, it always seemed that people were expected to be chatty and outgoing, but I am not. As well as this, I can't cope being around other people for long hours; and I don't like time used up that could be spent on my hobbies. Whenever I've had a job in the past, I find it extremely annoying that I have to fit my weightlifting around my job - I would much rather fit my job around weightlifting (which is what I do now and life is so much better).

Asperger's Syndrome does not have to stop you from getting a job. Sadly 80% of adults with autism are unemployed yet most are willing and able to work! We tend to be exceptionally good at certain things, such as numbers, organisation, things that require looking at data, editing reports and whatever else. If you can get a job that utilises your skills, you'll probably do really well and enjoy it.

When I was about 20, when asked about working, I quite bluntly said that I did not want to be employed because I was "too arrogant" to work for someone else and "too lazy" to commit to things that were not a priority for me. These were immature and blunt statements and no doubt came across as cocky! Now I'm older I think that what I was really trying to say was that I feel stressed in the workplace whilst also feeling bored. I am able yet can't cope with the demands of employment. I love how Asperger's Syndrome has made me dedicated, hard working and focused, but I find it a disability when it comes to actually getting or maintaining a job.

I've experimented with a number of different things. I've worked as a project manager in a chemical laboratory, a web developer, an internet marketeer, an assistant chef, a carer for the elderly, a veterinary assistant, and a newspaper deliverer.

Out of them all, my favourite job is my newspaper round, which I've been doing for many years with no intention of giving it up. I love cycling around on my own very early in the mornings. It's peaceful and beautiful. I'm on my own, in control of how fast I do it or which route I choose to take. See this illustration:

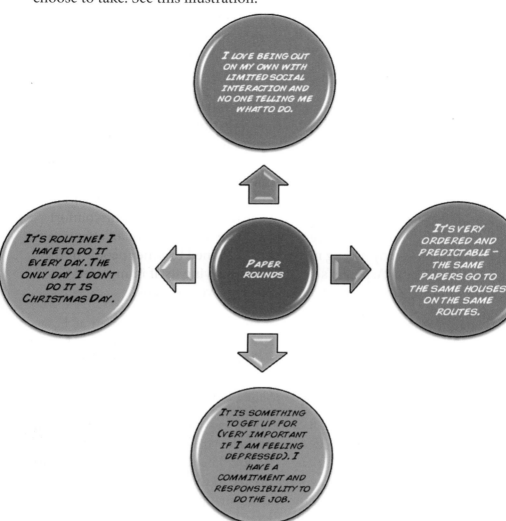

It does not quite fit in with my first class degree and masters in chemistry, but I am happy and relaxed.

I'm not a social person so it's a bit ironic how, at the time of writing, I've been a self-employed social media marketeer for 4 years! This means I have to "socialise" and communicate with people on the internet every day. I manage multiple social media accounts, which means I have several different "personalities." These personalities are extremely easy to characterise, I guess it's sort of like creating characters in a story. It takes near-zero energy for me to communicate online because the awkward barriers of body language, social anxiety and sensory challenges are gone. Social media is another way of "watching" how people communicate, and I find it very helpful, easy to follow conversations and learn what's currently in the news.

I've always known that I work best independently, so being self-employed has been really good for me. I do not enjoy working as part of a team. I'm aware there are advantages to teamwork, for example some people might be better at certain things than me and, generally speaking, the more minds there are the more likely a good idea might arise. Having Asperger's Syndrome has made me **extremely precise** so if I'm working as part of a team project, it causes me anxiety and discomfort because I feel that my colleagues won't have the same level of attention to detail. I don't enjoy having my work constrained by other people in the team. This is my Asperger's Syndrome displaying itself in my need for control of my environment, otherwise I feel very stressed.

A lot of people with Asperger's Syndrome suffer from social anxiety and yet also want to be the boss and do as we wish. This can prove itself to be a bit of a conundrum in team work situations because we have lots of good ideas, yet they often never get heard! We may then suffer in silence and feel extremely stressed, frustrated and unhappy with the situation.

At university there were a lot of times we had to work in a group. It was always something I dreaded. As well as the stress of communicating, I was also anxious that my final grade would be restricted by my ability to work in the group, or by the other people in the group. I have a very particular style of working and it means that projects are done in the most efficient, logical way, to the highest standard. I feel that other people won't meet my standards. It is not because they aren't conscientious or organised, or not good at writing, it's just because I have my own standards and I know exactly how to meet them. I have my own ways of finding journals, writing reports, my own way of making sure the work is finished well before the deadline etc. In addition to this, I am shy and find it hard to communicate effectively in a group.

Generally I am quite a submissive person so in a group environment, I will let someone else take the lead even when I'd prefer to be the one in control. This is very frustrating and stressful.

If you're planning to do any sort of higher education it might be very useful to contact your lecturers well in advance to explain some of the ways in which you work, which might be down to your AS. Difficulty working as part of a team may be one of these.

Socialising at work and with colleagues

In most jobs, it seems to me that it's important to be flexible, outgoing and assertive. I am none of these things - already I'm at a disadvantage at interview and in the workplace.

I've really liked most of the people I've worked with but, despite that, my preference was to always be alone. I've struggled in jobs primarily because of the social interaction involved. Even though my jobs haven't been particularly people-based (I've worked on computers and in labs) there's always a certain degree of social effort that is required.

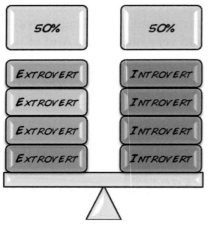

Unfortunately for me, the people I've worked with have always been very friendly and close-knit and have always really enjoyed going for drinks after work or having office parties, etc. They invite me but I just can't manage this. It's so hard to explain that I like them but can't socialise with them in this respect. I am similar to many introverted people, but my stress goes **off the scale** and can last days!

Based on my working experience, I now have my own theory about the population dynamics of introverts and extroverts in the working environment, which is demonstrated in these diagrams. The first one shown above illustrates one of the most common patterns - half of the people are extroverts and half are introverts.

I could not find a reliable source but many sources on the internet suggest that there is roughly a 50:50 split of introverts and extroverts in the world. In big teams, this will probably show itself very clearly. So if there are social activities out of the office, an equal number of people will and will not attend. In large groups maybe it is not noticed whether you attend or not.

On the other hand, if you work in a small team, you might find you are the only introvert and consequently there may be extra pressure for you to attend these social events. You might feel a bit of an outsider. And if you have Asperger's Syndrome as well, this feeling is magnified!

I have worked in this type of environment as well. The left diagram illustrates how it was. Because there were only a small number of us and everyone else was very extroverted, the social differences between myself and my colleagues was very big and very noticeable. And of course, because I am an introvert in addition to having Asperger's Syndrome, the social differences were even greater! Here is the diagram on the right.

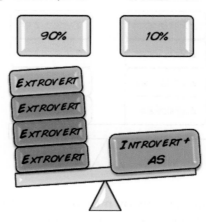

In the most ideal circumstances, I would like to be part of a team where there were a lot more introverts than extroverts; because then the diagram would look like the one on the next page. It would be a lot easier for me to work with people who were also introverted - it would be easier to explain to them that I prefer quiet nights in, rather than evenings at the pub with everybody else. I imagine it would be more "acceptable" to be a part of this team and that I would feel less of an outsider. These dynamics however, may not suit the extrovert - who might find it very quiet!

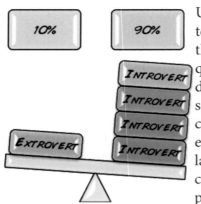

Unfortunately I have never been part of a team where there were more introverts than extroverts. In hindsight, I am actually quite surprised. The jobs I've had have definitely not been people- or customer-service based, so I would've expected more colleagues to have been introverts. For example, I have worked in a chemical laboratory, and in a web design/SEO company. But I also understand that people often put on their own "masks" for work and that they will sometimes force themselves to appear more outgoing or social than they really are. My theory or perspective might therefore be skewed. It is only a theory. I can only hypothesise based on my own experiences.

In one job, it was office tradition to go out for a staff meal every Friday lunchtime. The idea was to take turns in being the team member who had to stay in the office to man the phones, but I always opted to do it, just so I could avoid the dreaded social lunch! It also meant I had an hour of peace to myself in the office, in the middle of a busy workday. I probably attended just one staff meal in the whole four months I was there! I wondered if anyone realised why. Hopefully they just felt I was being helpful.

In less structured working environments, it can be horrible for the person with Asperger's Syndrome who is expected to drop their task in an instant in order to work on something more urgent. We tend to be very singly-focused and good at doing one thing at a time, to a very high standard. It is easy for us to get totally absorbed in whatever we are doing. Moving us on to other things all the time can cause meltdowns.

I've had trouble maintaining jobs because I get fatigued having to wear my normal mask at work. It's exhausting to always be polite, chatty, friendly and to act like you're never having a bad day! There are always expectations at work; some common ones are: shake a hand, wear smart trousers or participate in a team meeting. But work is stressful enough, with all the sounds and smells and lights, without additional social effort. A lot of the time I just want to curl up in a ball under my desk with my hands over my ears to try and block out the world (it's my way of coping, I do it a lot at home).

Like many other people on the autistic spectrum, there are also numerous other "things" that I have to try and manage:

- **Fidgeting**. I can't sit still. I have to get up every fifteen minutes, because I'm really fidgety and need to move around. In my last job, I used the excuse that customer orders needed to be posted so that I could leave the office and make trips to the post office every day (sometimes twice)
- **Spinning**. I have to hold back from spinning on my chair if it has wheels. It's a natural instinct
- **Noise**. I have to wear noise-reducing earplugs. Normal sounds are exaggerated. When I was at work, people were always talking or the radio was constantly blaring. Wearing earplugs can make me appear very quiet, distant and uninvolved from everyone else
- **Lunches**. I eat the same food at the same time every day and made "silly" excuses to avoid going out for lunch with the rest of the team, just because I didn't want to have to change my routine. I'd tell them I had work to do and needed to stay in the office. This might have made me seem very unsocial or that I had disordered eating habits (maybe I do to an NT!)
- **Frequent task changes**. Being moved away from a task on to something else. If I'm in the middle of working on a certain task, I feel very angry and upset because I am more suited to focusing on one thing at a time. I cannot just shift attention that easily.

It always takes a huge effort to have a conversation with other people, who seem to find it effortless. One of my most awkward questions to be asked is, "did you have a good weekend?" or "what did you do at the weekend?" Usually I'll just respond with a simple "okay thank you, how was yours?" to avoid giving anything away; but when probed I feel shy describing some of my interests because they're quite specific and I do not tend to do the things other people do at weekends. For example, it takes a lot of time and effort for me to explain to someone about the 'Clean and Jerk' if they don't know anything about weightlifting! I do not know how much detail they want to hear and I worry that I have misread or bored them. I'm very absorbed in my hobbies but I'm also aware that other people might not be as interested in them as I am. I'm conscious not to bore them with excessive detail but I worry that once I get started I won't be able to stop talking.

I love the weeks leading up to Christmas because everyone is always in a happy mood; but I dread the expectation that everyone will be going to the staff Christmas party. Sometimes I really try and make the effort to go, but once it backfired and caused me to have a shutdown; now I feel I can never go to a work party again. This is what happened:

THE GO-KARTING CHRISTMAS PARTY

We were going to go to Greenwich for indoor go-karting starting at 8.00pm and finishing at 9.00pm. After that, we were going to have a meal in a nearby restaurant.

I made a huge effort to attend the party. I decided that it'd be best for all of us if I made a compromise and only attended the first half of the party (the go-karting). In my head, although there were a lot of things I wouldn't like about the go-karting, mostly the travel, the talking and that it was taking place in the evening, I would probably enjoy the go-karting. I knew that my colleagues would enjoy it if I came. I thought it was a reasonable compromise.

But, what actually happened was, although I'd told them in advance I'd only be coming for the go-karting and that I had a taxi booked to pick me up at 9.00pm, I was socially pressured into staying beyond that for the meal. I even told them that I'd pre-paid the taxi, but they would not take no for an answer. I realised later that they only meant well but, at the time I felt stressed and pressurised. I felt that my great effort to attend half of the party hadn't even been appreciated. On the other hand, at that time, I had not been diagnosed and so they would not have understood why it was so awful for me.

I don't know much about some of the mainstream things that other people seem to mainly find interesting and appealing. For example, a colleague was really surprised to discover I had no idea who Paul O'Grady (a popular British television presenter) was. "Doesn't everyone know him?!" she said. I do try to keep up to date with things and occasionally I'll check the BBC website or glance at the headlines in the newspaper (one of the benefits of doing a paper round every day!), but I find it all very meaningless...

University

University was hard as well, especially at the start. Although I hated school, I really enjoyed my A levels and, at 18, I really wanted to go to university. I decided to embark on a chemistry degree, purely because a) I loved the subject and b) I was good at it. My parents and I also came to the conclusion that science students might generally be quieter and more studious than others. I didn't think much about the career this might lead to, I just knew that a science degree was a very useful qualification and taught many transferable skills. After lots of discussions with my parents we decided chemistry would be great for me and it might be easier to get a job having studied the subject, rather than studying computer science or English (other interests of mine). After all, at the time female chemists were quite unusual and scientists in general were in demand.

It wasn't a big consideration at the time, but now I see that typical chemistry-type jobs often lead to working independently. I would always have been more naturally drawn to working in a laboratory, or being a lone researcher, rather than working in sales, retail or other jobs that have a large social element.

You need to do what's best for you. After all, you're the one who's going to be part of university life for 3 or 4 years! Think about how you'd cope with busy rush hour travel. If you plan on going to a university far away, think about how you'd cope living with strangers in a new environment. Do you know how to pay bills? Do the laundry? Ask yourself whether you feel confident enough to look after yourself.

The entry/admissions process wasn't an easy one. At my college, there was a lot of prejudice and stereotyping about the status of different universities. I felt extremely pressured by teachers and other students to choose certain universities and consequently I applied to some of the top, prestigious universities in London. Although I received some offers I turned them down in favour of my local university. Choosing a university was always a simple choice for me - it was simply the nearest one to home. It was never a thought I'd move away from home. Just the idea of living in a new, unstructured environment full of students was unbearable. I always knew I'd have to commute because I just needed the solitude, security and familiarity I had at home. The shorter the commute, the better.

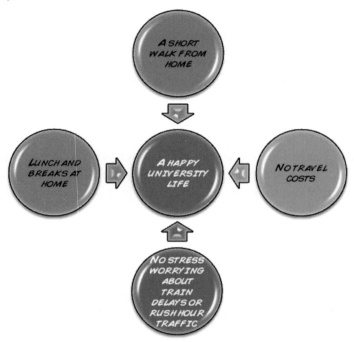

So even though my local university didn't have the reputation of some of the others, its location was most important to me. Simply put, being so close to home meant that I could get back to the familiarity, quiet and comfort of my own home very quickly if the day became too much. I could quickly escape for my all important rebuilding time.

After exhausting myself "fighting" off the insensitive comments from other people that I should have chosen a "better" university, I then proceeded to exhaust myself by worrying about what university would actually be like...

I think there is a lot of pressure for young people to go to university, but it's important to realise that university is definitely not for everyone. It would have been helpful for me if my teachers and college had been more encouraging about alternative options, such as open university courses, apprenticeships or internships. I don't remember these things ever being mentioned. It was assumed that everyone would go to university.

I carried out extensive research on forums on the internet, learning about real life experiences of students at university; but the stereotype of students - rowdy party animals who spent every waking moment socialising, drinking or flirting with the opposite sex - traumatised me. It seemed that for most students, degrees came second in favour of the crazy social scene. During the whole summer prior to starting term I was terrified of the preconception that everyone went to university to have lots of fun and make friends. Seemingly it was going to be one big party.

There was also little mention of a gap year. In my opinion, gap years could be really helpful to teenagers with Asperger's Syndrome. There is pressure on us to conform and be like our peers, even if we don't really want to. I know that I was very unsure of myself at this stage of my life. Developmentally, AS people have more to gain by delaying by a year or two. Remember we mature later than NTs of the same age. Just make sure you do something you enjoy that will help you to mature and grow in confidence!

I very nearly decided not to even go. I'm a simple person - all I wanted to go to university for was to get a good degree in a subject I genuinely loved! I enjoyed learning and wanted to continue with education, but I felt very alone in this thinking and consequently that summer was a very short (time passed very quickly because I was anxious) and lonely one. I must've worried about what the first day of term would be like every night that summer.

Eventually I decided that yes, I could probably make it through university, if I could just make it through the Fresher's Week. All the university material I read encouraged everyone to "get out there, say yes to everything, do everything, and just get involved and meet people!" What a nightmare for a socially awkward, shy, introverted Aspie like myself. All the advice I received told me to smile lots and portray myself as someone likable who was able to make friends really easily and "fit in."

I really did try to make an effort. The day before the first day of Fresher's, I repeated the conversations I thought would happen in my mind. I rehearsed saying yes every time someone invited me to do something. But when the day came I did my best to talk to people and I did appreciate them asking me to go out to pubs and clubs, but I ended up saying no to everything. I was just so worn out from the effort, I didn't want to wear the normal mask anymore. The first classes, the week after Fresher's, were very hard because I didn't know anyone.

My parents were very supportive and, receiving their love and help every day meant I was able to adjust to the university life more easily than had I lived away from home. I had their support and the comfort and structure of living at home, but I also had to be independent, by getting to university on my own and managing my workload.

In most ways though, I had an easier time at university than I did at school. I went to the classes I needed to, that was it. I think I was quite fortunate because many of my classmates still lived in their parental homes (like me) so I felt less left out. There were also several mature students who had families and, consequently they would arrive, learn and then go home. My reluctance to socialise was noticed less than it could've been, and I put this down to the sheer number of mature students or young people still living at home. These people did not attend many of the social activities, so I didn't always feel left out.

Appendix 1 shows a comparison of some of my experiences at school and university.

University is less regimented than being at secondary school, which means there are welcome breaks to rebuild. You are free to do what you want in your break times. It's okay to only attend for classes, although you might not feel okay doing this at the time. Looking back, it suited me.

8.
My Social Life

Social pressure

I've already talked about school and how wearing it was. The six-hours-a-day-five-days-a-week schedule was serious social overload. It's been the same with the jobs. I'm always really drained by the end of the day and just need to retreat into my own space when I get home.

I make an effort - I do always try to be a bit more sociable than I would naturally be. Every time I step outside of my house it's already outside my comfort zone. Inwardly, I am just not a social person and I enjoy mostly solitary activities. That I don't drink alcohol and am asexual also set me apart.

Unfortunately, for people with Asperger's Syndrome, planet earth is a social place - there's work, parties, family gatherings, shopping, medical appointments, even answering the phone or front door. Virtually everything that human beings do, see, touch, taste and smell, has a thought for, link to or impact upon, another person.

I do like the company of others (sometimes, but on my terms), but I also love and need my own company. I think sometimes people forget that just because they find socialising relaxing, it doesn't mean everyone else does! People who try to force social events on to me can make me feel the total opposite of relaxed; instead, I can feel very stressed! People will say things like this to me, "Come out with us and have fun! You need to let your hair down and socialise a bit." They don't realise that's exactly what I don't need.

> If you're not on the spectrum, I plead with you that when someone on the autistic spectrum says "no," they do mean no, so don't keep asking unless you want to give them a meltdown! I got tired of making up white lies about why I couldn't go out ("not feeling well," "sister's birthday."). Having a diagnosis and telling people that I have Asperger's Syndrome makes this a lot easier.

The main reason I was so desperate for my diagnosis was so that I could give other people an authentic explanation as to why I didn't socialise with them very often. It was always clear to me but I always felt that other people needed a more "qualified" reason.

I am better with one-on-one socialising rather than socialising in groups.

Whenever I am part of a group I tend to be very quiet and end up not joining in with the conversation, even with my family.

> I enjoy being with one person at a time. The mental effort and sensory challenges I experience are just about manageable with one person. Two is pushing it. Any more is just overload.

I was always aware I didn't have the same social energy "levels" as other people, but when I was younger I didn't know how to manage it. As an adult I've come to accept that I need that alone Alis time, my time to rebuild. I try to make sure I have alone time several times each day to enable me to manage my fatigue and reduce the likelihood of feeling socially "overloaded," which can lead to shutdowns or depression.

School, university and jobs have all made me feel socially pressurised. It is not a nice feeling. The thing is, I can recognise when someone means well or is trying to be nice. They can be kind and intelligent, but they can still exhaust me and hurt my feelings, without meaning to. I understand that people generally do mean well and are just being nice by including me in social situations. I think they just don't understand Asperger's Syndrome. And why would they, unless they have first hand experience? There is a sort of bridge between people with Asperger's Syndrome and others that needs to be created... or if it's already there, it needs to be finished. We just need to make connections.

When I was younger, I was too shy to be honest about why I didn't want to go to social events. My reason was always that I just did not want to go. Instead I used to mumble an awkward "maybe," "I'll see," or "I'll try and come." I felt really embarrassed. The reason "just not wanting to go" does not seem to have any meaning to people - but it is a very, very valid reason for me.

I dread receiving invitations to social things. I can cope with email or postal invites but telephone or face to face invitations are the worst, because it's a lot harder to say no when you're put on the spot. I do not like saying no to things; it makes me feel embarrassed and awkward and I always feel I'm letting the other person down. I feel emotions intensely and, from my viewpoint, I really hate upsetting someone, I spend a lot of my time worrying if I've hurt anyone. I wish I could make it more clear, or believable (is that the right word?), that just because I say "no," it doesn't mean I don't like you. It really does mean I'm too tired, don't want to or simply don't fancy it.

My personal reasons for not wanting to do things are extensive. It is hard to explain to a non-spectrum person these things. Here are a few of mine:

I SIMPLY WON'T ENJOY THE ACTIVITY, E.G. PUB, CLUB OR DANCING	THE TIME PERIOD DOESN'T SUIT ME, E.G. THE EVENT IS IN THE EVENING	THE EVENT IS IN AN UNFAMILIAR PLACE OR ENVIRONMENT FAR AWAY THAT REQUIRES ME TO TRAVEL BY PUBLIC TRANSPORT INSTEAD OF MY BIKE
THERE WILL BE LOTS OF TALKING AND A GOOD CHANCE I WILL HAVE TO MEET NEW PEOPLE	THERE WILL BE ALCOHOL INVOLVED; AND BECAUSE I DON'T DRINK I FEEL LEFT OUT. IT ALSO MAKES ME NERVOUS HOW OTHER PEOPLE ACT WHEN TIPSY	THE EVENINGS ARE MY FAVOURITE TIMES TO DO ALI'S THINGS
MY ROUTINE WILL BE DISRUPTED AND I WILL BE TIRED THE NEXT DAY	THE NEXT DAY'S ACTIVITIES WILL SUFFER THE CONSEQUENCE OF ME HAVING EXPENDED A HUGE AMOUNT OF ENERGY. MEANING I WILL BE TOO TIRED TO DO THE THINGS I NORMALLY DO AND LIKE	I AM NOT IN CONTROL OF THE SITUATION. E.G. OTHERS DETERMINE START AND FINISH TIMES, TRANSPORT HOME, CHOICE OF RESTAURANT ETC.

I also have trouble reconnecting with the majority of people who I have not seen, even if it's just been for a very short period of time. One reason is because I think they may have changed or be different from when I last saw them. Another reason is because I always feel a huge amount of pressure on me to tell them what I have been doing since I last saw them.

When I talk about myself to other people usually nothing much has changed because I am doing the same things that I had been doing since last time. Sometimes I think people don't believe me but, from my point of view there is nothing else to say. I experience a sort of internal pressure that I should be saying more. Even though I am doing the same things, they are always continually progressing. My hobbies are not static. For example, this week I am lifting more weight than last week. This month I am writing the end of my book and last month I was writing the middle. These are significant changes for me. Unfortunately, for a lot of NTs, these changes don't seem to be enough. Sometimes I feel they want me to say that I have been doing "bigger" things like they have been doing, e.g. going on holiday, seeing movies, or going to "central London" shopping (because a lot of people seem to prefer to go to central London to do shopping that could easily be done closer to their home!). These reasons together cause me a huge amount of social anxiety whenever I see people.

> For someone who has Asperger's Syndrome, I am quite socially aware. Therefore, I understand that many people do not want to hear the small detail and depth of my special interests, such as weightlifting or writing. The usual sort of social chat is very superficial, I do not feel it's appropriate for me to talk about what I've been doing to the extent that I want to. I would go on and on and give lots of detail. I find social chat unrewarding.

A typical conversation overleaf might be like this:

CARDIO AND PARIS

Them: Hi Alis. Where have you been hiding? Haven't seen you for ages!

Me: Hello. Yeah, I've been really busy. How are you?

Them: Good thanks. Busy doing what?

Me: Still writing my book. Still doing weightlifting. You?

Me (thoughts): It might not seem like a lot, to justify two months of not being seen, however I have made a lot of progress in this time. I am lifting 10% more weight and have written another 30,000 words. These are not easy achievements. They take hard work, discipline and a lot of time. They are more than enough to keep me busy and to justify not being seen for two months.

Them: ...Cool. I don't know how you keep up exercise, I find it so hard to go to the gym. Well, I've been to Paris with my husband. It was amazing. Busy at work.

Me (thoughts): They're not really too interested in what I've been doing, not to the extent I want to talk about. They just told me three big things (exercise, Paris, and work) and I want to hear about them in lots of detail, but they never give me enough factual detail. I want to know which airport they flew from, what time they arrived, how comfortable the hotel bed was, what time they arrived back, etc.

Having just read this conversation in hindsight, I've noticed that although I'm interested in finding out about their holiday, I am more interested in hearing about the things that would have been of concern to me. For example, when I go on holiday the things I am most concerned about include:

- Flight arrival and departure times
- What time I will have to leave my house in order to get to the airport
- Will I have time to do weightlifting before I leave my house

- How long the flight is
- How far the hotel is from the airport
- How I am going to get from the airport to the hotel
- How soft or hard the bed is
- How I am going to keep to my usual sleep and wake up routine
- Whether or not I will be able to eat the sort of food available
- What time I will return home and will I have time to do weightlifting when I get back, or will it be time for bed

I have spoken to my neurotypical parents about this. They have confirmed that, although other people are also interested in these things, they probably find them less interesting and would rather not have a full conversation about them. Instead, most people would prefer to talk about things, such as:

- The interesting and exciting food
- How cheap or expensive the local coffee bars are
- The gorgeous local men or women
- The beautiful accent
- How they wish they could retire and live there
- How less busy and so much cleaner it is than London or England
- The monuments and famous buildings
- How they only had a small amount of sleep because they were up late talking to and having fun with the local people

Unfortunately I am not really interested in these things, although I will try and listen when somebody talks to me about them - because I understand that these things are important to them. Having friends means taking an interest in things that are important to them, even if not to me.

Interestingly, I do not experience feelings of social pressure when I go to the newsagent each day to prepare for my newspaper rounds. This is because everyone is completely focused on getting the papers out and delivered. There is complete clarity of what everyone is doing and there are no confusing situations. There is no time for 'chit-chat' and no social expectation. We are all there to do a job.

I get stressed meeting new people or being in places that are too hot or which lack fresh air. In a previous job we moved rooms to go to the top floor. It was unbearably hot and I felt very stressed and was unable to concentrate.

The cafe that I go to has just changed its playlist. I have found it very hard to accommodate this change. Suddenly, the music is a lot louder and more boomy. The cafe used to play 'easy listening' neutral jazz music. Now, it is playing old pop songs. I have had to change where I like to sit, so that I can be far away from the speakers. I do not like hearing the pop songs. They make me feel very, very emotional. I have connections to songs, you can read more about this on page 193.

> Be aware that people with Asperger's Syndrome are extremely sensitive to their environment. This means that changes that may be minor to others, such as moving offices, can have devastating effects on us.

Loud noises or certain smells make me anxious. Long periods of time being around people are exhausting. I'm an early bird; my body clock runs from 4.00am to 8.00pm and I like to be at home winding down from my day after 3.00pm. The evening is therefore the perfect time for me to recuperate from the day's events, by writing or listening to audio CDs. If I don't have this time I feel as though I've "lost" myself, which can make me distressed.

> If you spend long hours around people, e.g. at work, make sure you have enough alone time in between your hours to recuperate. Never feel under pressure to attend social events after work. There seems to be an assumption that all people are social creatures but not all of us are. It doesn't mean there's anything "wrong" with you.

> I realise my inclination is to use the word "depressed" to describe a range of negative feelings. My emotional literacy is weak and I struggle to label my feelings with the colour that NTs add.

Every time I don't go to a social event, there's guaranteed to be an "aftermath" of comments, such as those in these speech bubbles:

IT WAS GREAT FUN, YOU WOULD'VE LOVED IT!

Since my diagnosis, I tend to just be honest

148

and straightforward and tell people the reason I won't go to a social event is because of my Asperger's Syndrome. Some people accept it, though there are a few individuals who appear to have a hard time understanding that no

means no and will continue to pester and ask me.

> This is one of the biggest benefits of having a diagnosis. Before I was diagnosed, I hated the fact that people didn't seem to accept "no" for simply the way I was/my personality. It was only when I had a diagnosis that it became "good enough" for people to accept. It was now a valid excuse.

Social energy levels
A life spent making choices

Everyone has 'energy.' I think of it this way - the two main branches of energy are: physical energy and social energy. For simplicity, let's say that each are worth 50% of the total energy, like this:

It's easy to explain what physical energy means and how to get it. It's what's used up during physical activity and can be regained by consuming food or resting. But what about "social energy?" In the broadest sense, I consider this to be all of the remaining energy. It is this social energy which has an impact on all areas of life - simply because we live in a "society."

For the majority of neurotypicals, it seems to me that they live a relatively smooth life. As I've mentioned before, they seem to so easily 'go with the flow.' Many people do not need to think much before they do something. For people with Asperger's Syndrome, **we always need to think before we do**. This thinking burns up our social energy. Others may need to think less or even not think at all, and their social energy tank remains full.

Here are some examples of things I use up social energy for:

- I wake up noticing that, for the seventh night in a row I did not sleep well due to temperature/noise/light. This means that I'm now at a low ebb and am wondering how I am going to cope with this shortfall of social energy for the rest of the day. I will have a threatening thought that today might be the start of a shutdown or even worse, the start of a depressive episode. Experience tells me they often come on due to lack of sleep
- The boss spontaneously drops it on everyone that we are going out for a staff lunch in the middle of the working day. Whereas everyone else seems to be able to "drop" what they are doing, I am preoccupied about the effect that this will have on the rest of my day. For example, I have already got my own lunch and don't want to eat anything else. I eat at 12.00pm and the table is booked for 1.00pm which means in hindsight that I should have eaten breakfast later, because I will be hungry. What time will we get back from the lunch and will I have to work later to make up the time? This means my whole evening gets disrupted. Lunchtime will use up a huge amount of social energy, leaving me with a very low tank for the rest of the day. This means that I will be unable to do other things

Little things that require no thought for others, such as going out to buy groceries, or taking the train to get somewhere to a work meeting, are **overwhelming** tasks for me, whereas for others I consider they are just day to day tasks.

What is considered one single task for other people, is broken into many little tasks for me. It is exhausting.

I've always known that my social energy levels were lower than other people's. My social energy tank is probably never completely full and even if it is, it empties quickly (maybe it has holes in!). So, here is my theory. To compensate for having a small social energy tank, I make a big effort to increase my physical energy every day. If I have lots of physical energy, it's more likely that my overall total energy will be high.

In this example my physical energy is full (10 bars of the total 10 available) and my social energy is less than half full (3.5 bars of the total available). My total energy is therefore nearly three quarters full (6.5 bars):

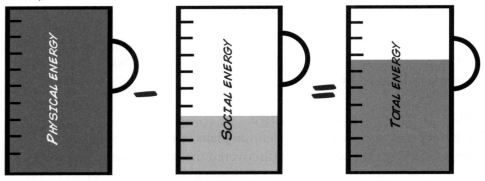

If my physical energy is low, for example I haven't been taking regular exercise or eating well, I slept badly, look at the impact it has on the total energy:

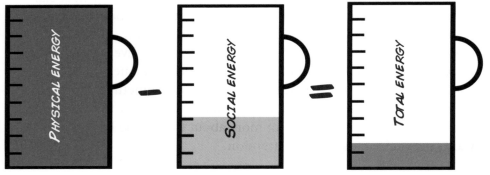

Physical energy is half full (5 bars), social energy is less than half full (3.5 bars). Total energy now is only 1.5 bars. I can't increase my social energy tank so, because of this, I have found it extremely helpful to keep fit. I exercise every day of the week, drink plenty of water, and eat a balanced, healthy diet. I also have a set sleep and wake time and always aim to get a good night's sleep. If for some reason my physical activities are curtailed, it has a huge impact on my mood. If my social energy tank is really low (say I have been having to socialise a lot) and I have not exercised, my total energy plummets. I have no reserve at all!

Having an exercise routine is easy to fit in to an Aspie's life. We love routine. Some form of exercise should be done daily, so schedule it in. It also gives you something to get up for, which is really important when you are feeling low.

This concept may not fit everyone. I do, however, truly believe that physical exercise is a huge benefit to anyone, AS or not.

Planning social meetings

It is very hard for me to make definite plans to meet up with people. Since writing this book, I have discovered the real reason why. When I meet up with someone socially, the ultimate decision of whether or not we meet is down to my social energy levels at the time.

Some people (extroverts) receive energy when they are in social situations. Others, like me, are introverts and expend energy in social situations. The combination of having Asperger's Syndrome and being an introvert means I get socially exhausted very quickly. All social interaction is exhausting, apart from with my family. Even with friends, I need alone time at the end of the day to refuel (imagine you've been driving all day and how you feel at the end of it). Sometimes it feels that I use up more energy spending time with friends, rather than strangers. I think this is because I care a lot more about the people I know and I want to give them my utmost attention.

So, even though I can make a plan to see someone, if maybe I've had an extremely socially energetic few days leading up to the event, I will probably need to cancel - simply because my social energy tank is empty!

It's better described by these social energy graphs shown on the following pages.

You can see that my social energy tank is full when I spend time on my own. Each time I do a social activity it causes my energy tank to decrease. It only fills up again when I have some alone time. Often, during the working week, I am so busy that there isn't really a chance for any kind of refill.

Therefore, by the time the weekend comes, I need those two days alone to regenerate some of that energy in time for the following week.

If a week has been less busy and less socially demanding, I will have more social energy to use up meeting my friends. However, if my social energy is low or zero at the time of meeting, I will be unable to see them.

This graph shows a typical working week (working Monday to Friday with weekends off):

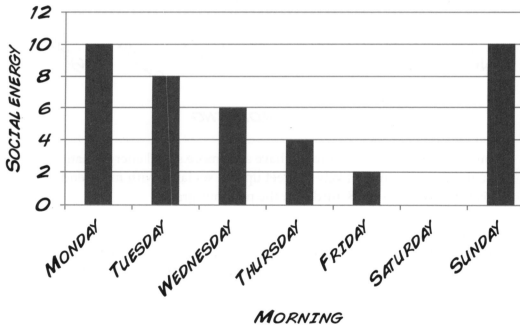

Look what happens if I take a day off work in the middle of the week (working Monday, Tuesday, Thursday and Friday with Wednesday and the weekend off):

SOCIAL ENERGY LEVELS DURING A WORKING WEEK (MONDAY TO FRIDAY) WITH WEDNESDAY OFF

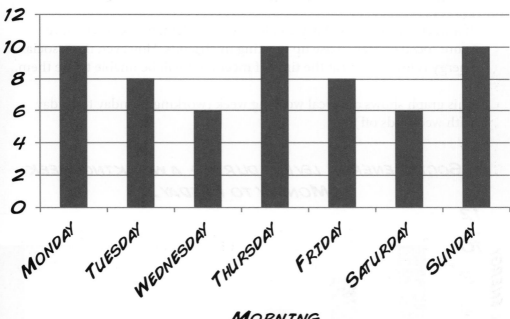

MORNING

You will notice that on Saturday I have a lot more social energy than usual. I would be more likely to meet up and socialise with my friends this Saturday, than the Saturday in the previous graph.

There are some weeks that will be so socially demanding that even before the weekend, my social energy tank has become zero. This is when it is likely a shutdown will occur. Look at this graph and see if you can follow what has happened:

SOCIAL ENERGY LEVELS DURING A WORKING WEEK (MONDAY TO FRIDAY) WITH SHUTDOWN

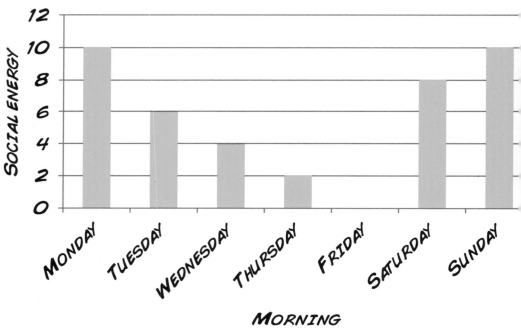

Monday, Tuesday, Wednesday and Thursday were just so socially demanding that by Friday morning I had no social energy left in the tank. It's important for me to take a day off work if this happens.

It is very hard for me to explain to others why I am like this but I hope these social energy graphs illustrate my feelings well enough to allow others to understand. I do not like letting my friends down by cancelling our plans at the last minute (particularly since I do not like this happening to me), but there is no real way of knowing how I am going to "feel" on the day, as to whether or not I can see them. Sometimes it is difficult, because I might like the person very much, yet I just won't have the energy to meet them.

It's very important to use my social energy on things that really matter, such as reducing energy spent working and increasing that spent on friends and partners...

> There's a well known phrase that says something like, "we give most of our time to people who are not worthy of it." For people with AS, take the time to reflect on this quote.

On occasions where I have to "be social" for long hours, such as when I was working in offices or at university, I've since learned that I need good sleep, as well as lots of down time in the evenings before and after these social days. These situations are very demanding and make me feel drained, agitated and stressed. I hate feeling this way and it lasts a long time afterwards. Even with positive experiences and outcomes, these feelings remain.

I have found most of my jobs to be too time-demanding. Most of them have required either long or inflexible hours. I cannot work in this manner, so I have found being self-employed and freelance better suited to me.

Social anxiety

My social anxiety is ubiquitous. I am generally shy too, which makes it worse. Social interactions, no matter how little, make me extremely anxious. I am a bit different from most people - I don't enjoy small talk, I don't usually find jokes that other people laugh at very funny. I get over stimulated by my environment extremely quickly and I enjoy being alone.

> I've heard that you can "become" socially anxious. Particularly when you are an adolescent, social anxiety may start presenting itself. The young person becomes aware that they are a unique individual who has their own mind, makes their own choices and is responsible for building their own relationships. When you are little, your parents can arrange for you to see friends and do things that children do. When you get older, you realise that you will have to make and maintain contact with others yourself. And you realise that how you behave socially will have an impact on all the future relationships you make.

I have learned, however, to be competent at being social. I can make small talk and laugh at jokes I wouldn't normally laugh at, just to fit in with the social situation. In everyday life, I pass at being "normal" 95%

of the time (I have built up and perfected a very good normal mask over many years).

> Often, autistic spectrum signs and symptoms become more prominent and difficult during adolescence. I've also heard that some girls don't even show any autistic signs until puberty! I imagine the combination of a) transition from the safe, familiar, cosy environment of primary school to the more complicated, variable and larger secondary school and b) all the hormonal changes going on during puberty, has an enormous impact on the social competency of someone with an ASD.

It's frustrating when sometimes social anxiety hinders potentially exciting opportunities. For example, I am very good at weightlifting. I have the opportunity to perform in competitions. However, I excel at weightlifting when no one is looking but can't do it when people are watching because I am so anxious about the venue, all the people, and the unpredictable (what if I don't achieve the lift?).

> For someone with AS, it is not always very helpful for us to be told to "just relax" or "take big, deep breaths and count to ten." AS people often have a lot of problems coping with anxiety and stress. We need to work extra hard to change our thoughts from negative to positive.

I get anxious whilst talking to people. I wonder what they might be thinking, but most often I question whether I'm making any sense. My conversations usually consist of numerous, "let me rephrase that," or I try and move the topic on to something my conversational partner is interested in. I can then just listen, even if I am finding the language hard to follow.

When I know I've got a meeting with someone the next day, I'll worry about it until it's been and gone. My ears get very hot and my racing heart rate may keep me awake at night. The best way for me to deal with this is to put on my lava lamps, self-massage and press my hands over my ears very hard.

Lifting weights is extremely stress-relieving, but I don't do it in the night! Finding and pursuing my hobby has been the best medicine for my anxiety.

Friends

I have a small number of friends and each one of them is a very special person in their own right! It's hard for me to maintain or develop a friendship unless the person is 1) understanding, 2) accepting and 3) at least somewhat knowledgeable about Asperger's Syndrome. For example, a friend must be comfortable only seeing me once every few months and understand that this is not an indication of how much I like them. Once this initial "challenge" is put out in the open, it is easier for both of us to maintain a friendship that has fewer miscommunications.

> As a friend, you should try and learn as much as you can about AS. People with AS experience the world differently, but we do care and we do have feelings. Even by learning about AS, misunderstandings can still happen, but please understand that we rarely ever intend to hurt anyone's feelings!

I imagine the traits of a good friend to be in a pyramid structure, like this illustration shows:

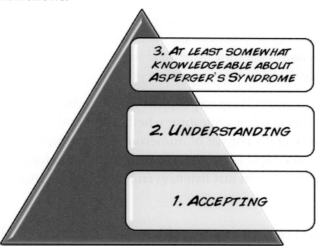

At the base of the pyramid - or the first thing the person should be - is accepting of my personality and my challenges. This means that they should be comfortable with certain things, such as only seeing each other once every few months or that our friendship will probably only ever be an early morning tea and a chat in my favourite cafe.

Next, a friend should be understanding, which means having sympathy and patience for someone who finds socialising very stressful and anxiety-provoking.

Accepting and understanding are a bit fluid, in that they overlap and depending on the situation. One trait may be more significant than the other.

Having some knowledge about Asperger's Syndrome is always really helpful. It helps us have less misunderstandings and reduces the chance of either of us getting hurt or offended. Some examples might be:

Situation	My thoughts and reasons	Their thoughts
I do not attend my friend's birthday party.	I am uncomfortable in social situations, particularly parties. I have magnified senses so things such as lighting and sound can distress me. It is hard for me to be around too many people simultaneously. I cannot follow multiple conversations easily.	It's a bit rude that she just decided not to come. Everyone else made the effort. She just doesn't care about me.
I have said, for example "You look rough today."	It's my Asperger's Syndrome just 'saying it how it is.' Sometimes I have trouble balancing my words with my meaning or intention. I do not mean to hurt or offend.	I feel extremely offended. That was extremely rude.

Situation	My thoughts and reasons	Their thoughts
My friend does not see me for several months.	I just haven't had the social energy. Usually it's because my social energy has been drained by compulsory tasks, such as going to work, rather than on seeing friends. If I had the choice, I'd rather spend my social energy on seeing my friend but work is a critical part of my life.	Have I done something wrong? Is she angry with me? Are we no longer friends? Maybe she doesn't really like me.
In conversation, I do not make eye contact with my friend.	Eye contact does not feel natural to me. It is not a personal attack. If I don't look people in the eye when they are talking to me, it's because my ears are doing all the work. I am listening very carefully, using the correct senses. If I look at the same time, it is harder for me to focus on the conversation.	Is she bored? Is this subject really that disinteresting to her? Is there something wrong with my face today that's making her look away?

The hardest part about friendships I find, is sustaining them. I have learned to be quite good at saying "hello" and introducing myself to someone for the first time but, it is much harder for me to know how to keep a relationship going. Sometimes the simplest reason is that I don't really know what we should do. I feel as though there's a pressure or expectation that friends are always supposed to be doing something, such as entertaining one another. In my experience, it's seen as a lot more "normal" to ask someone to hang out with you to see a movie, but less normal to ask just to "see" someone. A common response to this is, "Sure, so what will we be doing?" The honest answer is "I don't really know!" This is one of the reasons why I do not socialise much. I am happy just to be in someone's company and it's nice to find others who are like this too.

My closest friends now are people who I just see for chats and cups of tea. Sometimes we just both happen to be in the cafe at the same time or sometimes we are working. Sometimes we just sit near each other but not on the same table, reading separate books or working on our own projects. Every so often we'll pop over to the other's table for a little social break. But there is absolutely no pressure or expectation, which is so uplifting and I find these sorts of friendships extremely fulfilling. I have found them hard to come by. Is it just me or are people always looking to be doing something? I find it an enormous effort to always have to think up ideas on how to entertain someone.

My most successful friendships have been formed through very structured environments. For example, in college, university and work. We all have a clearly defined objective, whether that be to write a report, undertake a laboratory experiment or build a website. It is when this structure is missing, that I find continuing the relationship very hard. Outside of a structured environment, I just don't make an effort to keep the relationships going. I feel lost. Also, most of the time, the only thing I have in common with these people is the shared project, so when that's over, it feels as though there's nowhere for the friendship to go. This is sad, but makes me realise that the friends I have now are very special who will most likely be friends for life.

Sometimes I feel very sad that I am unable to experience pleasure from the same things as my friends. I love my friends and I love seeing them with smiles on their faces. They are good people. They always make the effort to invite me when they are planning something social, despite the fact they know I probably won't attend. More often than not, when I do attend, I feel like I just don't quite fit in. I don't seem to have the same fun that they are having. Even though I am included in conversations and activities, I always just feel that I am not quite fitting in. This is when I feel the glass wall between myself and the rest of the world most intensely. It is very sad. **I wish I could experience the same level of enjoyment that my friends experience; or I wish I could obtain pleasure from the same things that my friends get pleasure from**. I am comfortable with who I am and I love my world. But sometimes, I do wish I was able to enjoy my friends' worlds a bit more.

Being a little bit different, or 'atypical', is perfectly fine, but *it does* exaggerate my feelings of loneliness. I would rather not socialise to the extent that my friends do - it is physically and mentally exhausting trying to fit in and I always end up just wanting to go home. I imagine that introverts might feel this way in a group of extroverted friends. But I imagine that even though we experience the same feelings of being 'the outsider', my feelings are much stronger, my senses are overwhelmed and I am confused by multiple conversations.

If you care about someone with Asperger's Syndrome, it's always a good idea to invite them when you are planning something with friends. We might decline your invitation but it's a really nice feeling knowing that we were thought of and included. Never just assume that because your friend has AS that they won't appreciate an invite.

I do not like social expectation of any sort. I get very upset if someone knocks on my front door when I am not expecting them and I will not answer. It's the same with phone calls.

Though I like being alone, I also like sometimes just being around people. But I like being around people and my friends **without the pressure and expectation** to be talking or entertaining all the time. This is why I love our modern cafe culture - it's totally normal and okay to spend a whole day in a cafe if you want to, on your own, working on your laptop or reading a book. Nobody thinks you're strange and it's totally okay not to talk at all, except when ordering your drink (I don't even have to ask anymore, the waiters already know my drink!). It's also nice to see friendly faces, particularly if you're feeling sad that day. I have lots of local acquaintances and it's uncommon for me to go out without seeing somebody I know.

> Working in a cafe is quite a nice thing to do if you fancy it! Take your computer or your book, find a quiet table in the corner and bring earplugs and sunglasses to combat sensory challenges. Some cafes are even happy to serve you using your own mug. You can be social without actually being sociable. :)

I have noticed that my friends are very straightforward. I know where I stand with them and have learned to offer that same degree of being straightforward in return. It feels wonderful to be able to tell someone "I can't see you today. I'm socially drained and need to be alone," rather than make up something like "I'm busy tonight, it's my sister's birthday." And my friends will one hundred percent understand and accept this reason.

When I was younger in particular I found that there were things that felt natural to me that just did not feel natural to others - I am intuitively drawn to learning about things like recycling, pollution, animals, and social justice. Other people find things such as going on holiday a more easy form of social chit chat. It makes it hard to know what to talk about.

Forums and social networks

I don't physically meet up with my friends very often, but I enjoy building friendships and bonding with people on the internet, even though I have no real desire to meet them (I love my Facebook friends but would be overwhelmed to meet them all). I do not know anybody who shares the same enormous passion for weightlifting that I have, so weightlifting forums have given me the chance to explore and talk about this aspect of my life. I often feel that I have fulfilled the need of mine to talk about weightlifting, without boring my friends in minute detail that they would not understand.

Romantic relationships and love

When I was younger I was more flexible in my way of thinking and more open minded. In my "Conformation Years" it was easier to go dating than it is for me now. Those meetings might have been easier but, because of my normal mask, they were meaningless. I cannot go back to that mask and date people in the way that I used to - it uses up far too much of my energy. If somebody ends up falling in love with me, they will not have fallen in love with my true self.

Without my normal mask, it seems to be extremely hard to maintain a straightforward relationship; they've always been very confusing and baffling. Although I recognise that relationships are hard work and take a lot of time and effort, I continually find myself just unwilling to do the work to make the relationship continue through good and bad times. Instead, my solution has always been to just end the relationship. I feel that the effort, work and compromise involved hugely outweigh all benefits of having someone to be with. Most of the time I am happier and more comfortable when I am on my own. All of my partners have overwhelmed me by wanting more of my time.

I have had relationships with three NTs and one Aspie and each have had their own positives. I loved the understanding I had with my Aspie partner and my favourite thing about him was his creativity. He was extremely talented and much of his creative work was like magic. But I did not like his constant moaning and lack of empathy, which often came across as thoughtless or selfish. I do not know whether I am being hypocritical to say this, it's just how I feel. I am not patient enough to cope with another Aspie's "special needs," when coping with my own is already overwhelming.

The NTs, on the other hand, were flexible enough to at least make the effort to fit in with my lifestyle and routine, they were more carefree and easygoing, better at coping with my mood swings and generally more fun to be around. All three of them were very patient and accommodating. Although I treat everyone as an individual, from what I have seen and read of Aspie men, it would be hard for me to date another. I like NTs - but I don't think I could have a relationship with an extrovert. It would be too much.

I will enjoy being with someone for a time but then I need to go home and be alone for a day or several days and my partners have found this isolation hard to cope with.

If you are an NT, you might worry when your AS partner disappears for a few days and fails to contact you. Honestly, we don't usually have anything to hide, we just have to retreat sometimes. An NT who is unfamiliar with AS could easily jump to the wrong conclusions, such as their partner having an affair or that they have an addiction to something!

It's hard to explain because... I want to be with someone... **sometimes**. It is hard to find someone who will fit in with that.

Talk to your Aspie guy or girl and let them know that you'd appreciate a text or a photo every day. Even if they are busy, let them know that a small daily gesture to maintain contact, such as a simple text "goodnight" makes a huge difference to you in knowing that they care.

I've never had a partner who I met through day to day contact; all of them were met through internet dating. It's extremely hard for me to meet potential partners in day to day life. This diagram overleaf illustrates some of the challenges I face:

I FIND MEETING STRANGERS AND GENERAL SOCIALISING VERY STRESSFUL

MOST PEOPLE TEND TO BE QUITE "NORMAL" AND LIKE DOING NORMAL THINGS, SUCH AS GOING TO THE CINEMA, THE PUB, HAVING DINNER PARTIES OR REGULARLY MEETING FRIENDS. THESE THINGS PRESENT ME WITH CHALLENGES

THE PROBLEMS ASSOCIATED WITH MEETING POTENTIAL PARTNERS IN DAY TO DAY "REAL LIFE"

I DON'T HAVE MANY FRIENDS AND I DON'T SOCIALISE WITH PEOPLE MY OWN AGE

MY HOBBIES ARE SOLITARY AND TAKE PLACE AT HOME

MY WINDOW OF BEING AWAKE IS FROM 4.00AM TO 8.00PM SO I MISS OUT ON THE SOCIAL THINGS THAT HAPPEN IN THE EVENINGS

Then I discovered internet dating websites...

Internet dating

The most uplifting thing I found about internet dating was to be easily in control of who I spoke to or who I met up with. I suppose I treat internet dating like a "job interview;" I can express my preference for the desirable and essential qualities I look for in someone. It is easy for me to create a dating profile about myself. I feel I can be wholly honest (there is no normal mask). I've never shied away from openly stating that I don't like going out much and that I love my own space a lot of the time. I would rather someone know about this immediately, rather than have them find out later. Asperger's Syndrome is just so fundamental to who I am, and it can't be changed.

Reading the detail of another person's dating profile is an analytical process. I have to check what they've said for compatibility and incompatibility before I can even consider communicating with someone.

Here is an example of something that caused me mental chaos:

HAVE A LONG LIE-IN, BREAKFAST IN BED, SEE FRIENDS FOR A SUNDAY ROAST AND THEN WATCH THE FOOTBALL FOR THE REST OF THE DAY AT THE PUB

Someone once sent me a message on a dating site and it was clear they hadn't even bothered to read my profile. When I checked their profile, one question asked was "Describe your ideal Sunday morning." Their response told me that they had not paid attention to my own profile because I said that a) I was an early bird b) I had rigid eating habits and c) I don't like going out very much. I decided I wouldn't respond to their message.

Some people have said to me that by being so picky I'm missing out on meeting lots of "potentially wonderful" people, or that people will say anything online so long as it's what they think other people want to hear. If this is true, it seems bizarre to me... I must be in the minority; I prefer to be completely straightforward because I want my relationships to be truthful and open. Other people are confusing! It does not make sense to me to put on my profile that I like lie-ins on a Sunday morning just because I think that most people like lie-ins - and consequently, improve my chances of finding someone. It's important that I am explicit, for example, that I don't like lie-ins on a Sunday morning, that I wake up at 4.00am and do a quick cycle round the block. My life is routine-driven and rigid.

Even though I'm not a very social person face to face, I really do enjoy talking to people on the internet. In fact, it's usually more exciting talking to people online, rather than actually meeting in person. Emails and text messages are my favourite ways to chat. I like it that I'm able to take things at my own pace and can read a message as and when I choose.

When initiating communication on dating websites, within two or three messages, I'm able to know for sure whether the person will be compatible or not. I'm also very picky about proper English, so if someone writes to me using poor English or uses a lot of slang, they probably won't hear back from me. It is the "small things" that I find important. I think this justifies a comment! - my own English is not always correct but incorrect English in others I pick up on immediately. I am therefore not entirely sure I have a "right" to judge others by their English! I am a walking paradox.

Communication

The internet is, by far, my favourite way of communicating with the world. I actually quite like Facebook and Twitter, I suppose they're my substitute for spending "real" time with people. Spending time with someone doing something in real life is usually too much; and going to a party or a pub is way too much. On the internet, I can be sociable as and when I feel, it fits around whatever I'm doing and I can switch it on and off as and when I choose.

I enjoy keeping in touch with people and finding out what old friends or acquaintances are up to, but I'd usually rather not meet up in person. Facebook and Twitter allow me to have that casual contact, without any pressure. I don't post much on my own profile (I don't have the energy for that), but I'll mention things that I find important and I'll comment on someone else's post if I find it interesting.

I'm quite happy only seeing people once every few months. Social media, email and text messaging are perfect and I really enjoy using them. Unfortunately, I've found that most people don't always like this way of communicating and prefer meeting more regularly and using other communication methods less! I don't really understand why.

Problems "progressing"

I don't know how to "progress" as other couples do. It's the same with friendships, I just don't really know what couples actually do, particularly when one of them is on the autistic spectrum? I think, for me, having a relationship means enjoying talking to (texting) someone everyday and meeting up with them occasionally to have a cup of tea together. I do not crave the physical presence of someone; I probably enjoy them more without physically being with them. I guess I just want someone flexible, undemanding and stable. Stability is the most important thing. I'd like them to have lived in the same place for a long time or have a regular job. This tells me that they have a stable routine already established.

It makes me feel a bit sad to write this, but it's unlikely I'll ever live with someone or have children. I'm unable to travel distances to meet people. Sensory problems (loud noise, strong smells and bright lights) and social overload mean I would prefer not to attend parties or family gatherings.

There are times when I wish that having a relationship could be a "priority" for me, as it seems to be for a lot of people. I think - and intellectually, I know - my life would be easier, a lot more fun and a lot less lonely if I had a close partner or friend. Instead, my priorities are my hobbies (weightlifting) or any projects that I'm working on (presently, it's this book). Prioritising hobbies rather than people is really common for people on the autistic spectrum. I'm not romantically inclined and it does not seem sensible to put my social energy (which is already always lower than average) into something I never really wanted in the first place.

I've had a small number of relationships. They have all been different but the one common factor is that all of my partners have made me their "everything," even my Aspie one. For them, relationships were central to their world (my Aspie partner even got a bit obsessed with me) and a lot of their interests were pursued with only me in mind. For example, a partner wants to go to the cinema but he only wants to go with me; or he wants to visit a museum, but he'll only go if I'm there as well. Whereas I have a lot of other things on my mind, because all I want to do is write my stories or do weightlifting and I'm not overly "bothered" about being with them - as hard as that sounds. If I fancy going to the cinema I am happy to go on my own; I never feel I *need* someone else to be able to do something. I don't really understand this way of thinking.

Here is an example of how how one of my relationships became strained:

SEEING A MOVIE

There was a movie on at the cinema that we both wanted to see. We planned to see it on Thursday at 10.00am. On Wednesday evening I decided I didn't want to see it tomorrow, so I cancelled our plans. I'm sure he was disappointed, but I didn't know what I could do about this. I told him to still go and see the film if he wished to go, but his response was that he wanted to see it with me and wouldn't go alone.

A few days later I decided that I wanted to see the film. He was at work that day, so I went and saw it alone. He was upset but I did not know why - he could have seen it.

From my perspective: I wanted to see the film but, like many people with Asperger's Syndrome, I can change my mind in a split second. I have to be in the mood to do something and if I'm not, I just won't do it. There's a word for this, 'mercurial' - it means subjective to sudden or unpredictable changes. How contradictory that I thrive on order and planning, yet my mood is mercurial?

I realise that sometimes my thoughts and actions may appear selfish. I want someone to fit their life around me and not the other way round. I can't help feeling this way as this is how I am. I realise that people on the autistic spectrum do have to learn how to cope in a predominantly non autistic world. But it's hard... and overwhelming...

Sometimes there really is no reason other than "I don't feel like doing that today." People often find this 'excuse' too vague and hard to accept and understand. It can make them feel frustrated and angry.

Consequently I do not like to commit or make plans to do things which involve other people because I don't want to let them down if I change my mind at the last minute. I really hate upsetting people. I just feel I can't commit to social things because I just don't know how I'm going to feel until the last moment. I'd rather not make plans and generally prefer to do things on my own, because then it's only me that is affected should I change my mind.

In the situation above, I ended up really enjoying the film because I'd seen it in my own time, when I was prepared and ready. It was not my fault that he would not go and see it on his own. If I was him, I would have gone to see the film. Then he would not have missed out. Surely if someone wants to see a film, they should go and see it regardless? This is a really key AS-NT difference.

Sometimes I feel that I actually enjoy pursuing an interest more if I am alone rather than with someone else. I enjoy going to the cinema on my own occasionally. I have total control over what film I see, the time of showing and the arrival time - I can arrive there just as it's starting rather than sit through the boring commercials. Plus, I don't have to talk about it afterwards!

I love painting on my own. Once, a partner asked if they could sit with me while I painted. They said they would not talk or disturb me, but quietly get on with their own work. But for some reason, I could not let them sit with me whilst I painted. It would have taken away all the enjoyment I got from painting. I have some interests where I definitely have to be alone in order to enjoy them. I cannot do that if anything is interrupting my enjoyment, if that makes any sense at all.

I have some other interests that I prefer to do on my own. Some examples of these are cinema and theatre outings.

In the early stages of some relationships, my partner could easily feel neglected, because he did not understand that I needed time on my own to pursue my hobbies. It was not the nature of my hobbies that caused him to feel this way, but the uncompromising, single-minded way in which I pursued them. For example, I would always pick weightlifting over seeing him, whenever I had free time.

Sometimes the only way to be is honest... if you feel that your NT partner demands too much of your time, reassure them that your need for space and time alone does not mean that you love them any less. When you are on the autistic spectrum, it is easy to feel overwhelmed.

I have had a long-distance relationship in which we only saw one another once a week. When my partner moved to live closer (just across the road!), we still only spent the same amount of time together, as we had when we lived a long way apart. He was neurotypical and he would've spent every day with me if he could! Even though I knew how hard he had tried to accommodate my ways, I sensed it was an uphill battle for him to completely overcome his expectations of a conventional, intimate relationship, particularly since he'd been very close to his previous partners. We talked about our feelings and tried to work out how we could make the relationship more enjoyable for both of us. I wanted a friend, whereas he wanted a girlfriend - we compromised on having a friendship most of the time and emotional and physical intimacy some of the time (but only when I was in the mood for it). We tried to work on our relationship in this way, but it didn't take long for me to realise that the reality of actually being with someone and being... "constrained" to the shackles of a permanent relationship is too stressful for me.

> I say "no" to going out, doing things or being intimate a lot. An NT person unfamiliar with Asperger's Syndrome might feel offended or frustrated. But with time and lots of reading, they will get accustomed to it.

At 24, I wonder whether my partners ever just feel physically and emotionally exhausted, because of the amount of work required by them to keep life on track for both of us... My partners can easily become my shock absorbers. They will soak up all my anxieties and feelings of stress and sadness. But consequently it is easy for their own lives to become drained.

I wonder, if I ever did get married, whether it would be out of practicality and "convenience" for my own needs, rather than for loving and fulfilling the emotional needs of my partner. It would be really handy to have someone to share the bills and someone always there to help me load the barbell for weightlifting. I'd actually really like the lifelong companionship with someone else, but it's never been a priority of mine and I'm worried my other half would feel "disappointed" or "trapped," or even somewhat "betrayed" by our contradicting views on what a marriage is and what it means.

An AS/NT relationship will be unconventional. There will be contradictions and paradoxes but the relationship can still be a good one. I do not often show or tell my partners how I feel. It is very hard for me to express my love for someone, but if I get on well with them, they will know deep inside that I do. Sometimes the AS needs to remember to externalise their internal thoughts.

There'd be so many sacrifices and so many things we'd be unable to do as a couple - nights out, holidays, festivities, even sharing a bedroom. They would all have limitations. If I do too much socialising, I will "pay" for it the next day. I imagine it feels sort of like a hangover (very muggy-headed, exhausted, sick, worn out). Sometimes it will cause me to end up shutting down, or even worse, the beginning of a depressive episode. I have never had a hangover but I imagine that might be a good metaphor for non-spectrum people to understand.

I like the idea of having a partner who I could see occasionally whilst living and sleeping separately. I know what I like and what I don't like. I have a strong sense of individuality and identity, but this also makes me very rigid, inflexible and unwilling to compromise. For example, it would be very hard for me to move if my partner got a job somewhere else.

I would also like it if my partner took an interest in my hobbies, but then it's hard for me to take an interest in what they do. I would like them to help me with my weightlifting but I wouldn't want to watch them play football. It's not so much the watching bit, it's all the stuff that comes with it - the travelling, the unfamiliar sports field, the crowds, the socialising etc. Maybe it would be okay if my partner liked something that required less social effort, for example if he was a writer then I would love to read his writing - or if he was an artist I would like to look at his art. But both writing and artwork are things I'm interested in. It's common for people with Asperger's Syndrome, that if there's something we don't really enjoy, it's a lot more difficult for us to show our interest.

You might experience this differently. Are you able to take a genuine interest in your partner's hobbies, even if they don't interest you?

It is imperative to me that any partner of mine takes a lot of time and effort to fulfill their own social needs, because there are many times where I will be unable to fulfill them. I have always encouraged my partners to go out with their friends, or see any movies they really want to see, even take holidays without me. I am also open to the idea of a polyamorous relationship, so that they could still enjoy sexual intimacy. I do not want to be responsible for "holding someone else back."

A person in a relationship generally has three types of needs: 1. Emotional 2. Social 3. Sexual. In an NT/NT relationship usually all three types are fulfilled. In an AS/NT relationship, one or more of their need types may be unfulfilled for the NT. It is important the NT finds ways to ensure their own needs are being met.

One partner became extremely bored with my preference to only ever watch one T.V. series. Even though we'd seen all of the three hundred episodes before, I still really enjoyed them. I remember the tone of his voice, as well as his words, "but we've seen them all before. They always show the same ones." He wanted to watch other things, but I didn't.

It's become clear to me that sharing a house with someone would be extremely difficult because, when I am tired, it is debilitating to even just 'be' around people. It would be hard for me to share a house with someone, let alone a bedroom, because I feel I'd "lose" my individuality. Living with someone, for me, means compromising and having less alone time. Would our house have to be as we both wanted it? But what if my partner wanted yellow walls and I hated yellow walls? I need to have blackout blinds but what if they loved light rooms and morning sunlight? I like to have lots of sensory lighting and lava lamps, I hope they'd like them too. I worry that some or all of my needs would have to be compromised.

Always give each other space. It will help keep the spark glowing and you'll never run out of things to talk about! :) And keep communicating with each other. If you are the AS, reassure your partner that you never forget them, even when you're not together. Let them know how important they are to you. If you are the NT, read as much as you can about Asperger's Syndrome and talk to your partner about their own experience of it. It can be hard to describe how things affect us or to know whether our feelings and behaviour are because of our AS or whether they're just normal! The more you read, the better you'll become at asking questions and your partner will become better at answering them. As a result, you will be able to compromise a lot more. Understanding on both the NT and Aspie's part is the foundation. Once that's done, the ability to communicate and explain things becomes much easier.

Also, it's likely that we would have disturbed sleep because I like to wake up early at 4.00am and go to bed very early at 8.00pm. I have problems sleeping in the same bed with someone else. There are just too many sensations going on at the same time. Even if they are quiet and being still, I am still extremely aware they are there. I don't like feeling like I cannot stretch out my leg because, if I do, it's going to touch someone else. I don't like having to sleep to one side only because, if I turn over, my face will be near theirs and I will experience their breathing. I find sleeping with someone else to be very claustrophobic and restrictive. My bed is a private space where I can just "be" and when that space is shared, I can no longer be, it's like the mask comes on again. I do not want to not be myself.

You need to be a certain type of person to be part of a 'mixed' AS/NT relationship. There are probably the same number of issues from both the NT and AS side that cause a relationship to fail. I can only speak from my own experiences but, most NTs cannot cope with the challenges of a relationship with someone who has Asperger's Syndrome. There are problems in an AS/NT relationship that simply are not encountered in an NT/NT relationship. The key is to find the right person for you! You love someone for their personality, which includes any quirks or diagnoses. Differences in neurology is just a part of that.

9.
Depression

Asperger's Syndrome - my comorbid condition

Unfortunately it is extremely common for people with Asperger's Syndrome to also have depression and anxiety challenges. Ever since puberty I've had periods of feeling just totally mentally exhausted, sad and empty; and I've had periods where I've had little interest in things I used to love doing. I've also had some very dark thoughts about death.

Asperger's Syndrome often has what are known as 'comorbid' conditions, meaning there may also be lots of other issues going on. Studies have been done to check for correlation between AS and mood disorders.[1] In particular, girls with ASD are more likely to be susceptible.[2]

1 Tantam, D. (2000). The Prevalence of Anxiety and Mood Problems among Children with Autism and Asperger Syndrome. Autism. 4 (2), 117-132.
2 Solomon, M., Miller, M., Taylor, S., et al. (2012). Autism symptoms and internalizing psychopathology in girls and boys with autism spectrum disorders. Journal of Autism and Developmental Disorders. 42 (1), 48–59.

Some of the Aspie reasons for my long-term, ongoing depression are:

LOW SELF ESTEEM DUE TO FEELING UNACCEPTED AND MISUNDERSTOOD

UNSATISFACTORY RELATIONSHIPS WITH PEERS

FEELINGS OF EXTREME LONELINESS

BEING BULLIED

BLACK AND WHITE THINKING, FOCUSING ON THE EXTREMES

Growing up and reading a lot about Asperger's Syndrome and depression has improved the way I cope, and now I can say that depression is something that I have accepted as a part of me and have learned to live with it. This does not make it easier but has made it understandable. When I was little, I had little knowledge of Asperger's Syndrome, I did not have any real reason for my depression, which made me feel worse. I remember wondering why I felt just **so bad**, even though my life was generally so positive? I had a wonderful family. We had a really comfortable home and lived in an affluent area. We had some lovely animals. I did well at school. I had a few nice friends. I was really good at writing and drawing. Yet in spite of all these positive things, I still felt so low! It did not make sense. As I got older, I was determined to find answers to the endless questions I had about why my life was so different to other people's lives. Asperger's Syndrome has answered all of my questions.

> We have a very cognitive way of thinking - we need facts and reasons for everything. Simply having knowledge of Asperger's Syndrome has the power to change your life by making you realise you're not so alone after all. Read as much as you can about it and seek a diagnosis if possible.

Since my diagnosis, everything has made sense. I have a reason for why my life has been this way... for why I've been so unhappy.

Triggers
Doing too much

Probably one of the biggest triggers for my shutdowns, which sometimes lead to depression, is simply doing too much. Since realising this, I've learned that to optimally "manage" my fatigue it's best if I only do one, single, planned, thing every day. The best way for me to explain this is to show you the differences in an "Alis Week" now and an Alis Week in the past.

> To the neurotypical, this might seem like an inefficient way of living. It often means that I can only do up to 5 social activities per working week. However, my social energy levels are less than the average person. I have to adapt my lifestyle to keep myself fit and well. We all have triggers and this is one of mine.

Let's say that the following activities need to be achieved in one week:

1. Meeting A
2. Doctor appointment
3. Personal training session
4. Seeing a friend
5. Meeting B
6. Meeting C

An Alis week now (Week 1)	
Monday	Meeting A
Tuesday	Doctor appointment
Wednesday	Personal training session
Thursday	Seeing a friend
Friday	Meeting B

An Alis week in the past (Week 2)	
Monday	Meeting A + doctor appointment + seeing a friend
Tuesday	
Wednesday	Personal training session + Meeting B
Thursday	Meeting C
Friday	

Can you see the difference?

Even though Week 2 clearly has two empty days (Tuesday and Friday), Week 1 is a much wiser and safer way for me to arrange my activities. There is only one planned, social, event on each day. Notice however, that in this arrangement there is no space for Meeting C. I would either rearrange it to happen the following week or, if it was urgent, I would swap it around with one of the other activities.

In Week 2, although Tuesday and Friday are empty, Monday and Wednesday are too busy and would most likely cause overload. I'd probably end up shutting down. This may consequently mean that activities on Wednesday and Thursday have to be cancelled.

All the things that aren't in my usual routine have to go into a diary like this. Things like doing my paper rounds or going in the gym are usual and mandatory and won't be changed for anything. They are the things I enjoy doing and that form part of my identity.
I remember, when I first started dating I had a real problem trying to communicate to people that I was only able to meet them for a single

hour to have a cup of tea. A lot of them wanted to spend the whole day doing multiple things. For example, one boy I met suggested we should meet up for a cup of tea, then go to the London Aquarium, followed by a meal afterwards. I'm sure that he meant well and simply wanted to make sure I had a good time but, it was just far, FAR too much. The outcome was, we met for a cup of tea, but I made sure he knew prior to our meeting, that I only had one hour free. Unfortunately at the time I had to lie and tell him I had other commitments after seeing him, because I didn't feel I could adequately explain that "I can only do one thing a day." I'm older now, and more comfortable telling people the real reason.

Doing too many things (whether they be the same things or different things) basically just exhaust me! All "things" involve challenges. Common ones are travelling, keeping to time, loud noises, strong smells, crowds, other people and working out what they are saying, unfamiliar places - there's an endless list. Life in general just has too many things going on at the same time. If I am seeing someone, I want to focus my attention fully on their company. I think that's fair enough.

I've come to the conclusion that, if I have to do any form of socialising, depending on who it is, it's best for me to just meet them for a cup of tea. Having a cup of tea with one person is more than enough stimulation. If you add anything else to the equation (e.g. a movie, a party or a game of tennis) I feel totally over stimulated and exhausted. I'm quite "basic" in that it doesn't take much to over work my mind. A cup of tea for one hour is the best thing. Unlike some other people, I do not get "bored" with my friends - tired yes, but not bored - seeing someone is always like seeing them for the first time, every time. Actually, I do not find the human race boring at all. Human psychology, feelings, behaviour and emotions are some things I find the most interesting. I believe that there is so much to be explored in any individual.

Stress

Because I am so sensitive, even something as "minor" as getting to bed two hours later than usual, sleeping through my alarm clock, or getting a sudden puncture in my bicycle tyre, can do considerable damage to my functioning and make me feel extremely stressed. As single things, they are minor - but they have the ability to disrupt a whole day's routine. When I am stressed, I notice that my "negative" emotions become a lot more exaggerated. It must be Asperger's Syndrome which makes them so much more noticeable. For example, I can very quickly become extremely sad or lonely. I stim a lot more. I cry out of the blue. Some people comment that I look "out of it."

Stress causes meltdowns, shutdowns and sometimes depression. I try and remove as many stressful influences in my life as I possibly can. Something like simply doing too much, as described above, can stress me to the point of depression. Stress is a huge trigger for that and if I am stressed for too long a time, I am highly likely to get overloaded, become completely socially withdrawn, unproductive, and consequently depressed.

For many people with AS, daily life is an exaggerated version of normal life.

Here on the next page are just a few of my own personal stressors and my management strategies:

DOING MORE THAN ONE THING A DAY	• I HAVE TO PLAN MY WEEKS IN ADVANCE AND MAKE SURE I ONLY HAVE ONE SOCIAL COMMITMENT PER DAY.
HAVING TO MISS A SESSION IN THE GYM	• I TRY AND MAKE SURE THIS NEVER HAPPENS. IF, FOR EXAMPLE, I AM AWAY FROM HOME FOR ONE FULL DAY, I PREPARE IN ADVANCE TO HAVE THAT DAY AS A REST DAY FROM THE GYM. IF I KNOW BEFOREHAND THAT I'M GOING TO BE RESTING, I FEEL BETTER ABOUT MISSING A DAY.
GOING TO BED TOO LATE	• I TRY NOT TO GO OUT IN THE EVENINGS BUT, ON THE OCCASIONS I HAVE TO, I LET PEOPLE KNOW I WILL NEED TO LEAVE EARLY.
RECEIVING AN EMAIL FROM MY BOSS	• I LIKE EMAILS BUT FOR SOME REASON, SOME WORK EMAILS MAKE ME FEEL VERY ANXIOUS. MY FIRST THOUGHT IS ALWAYS THAT I'VE DONE SOMETHING WRONG AND I'M BEING TOLD OFF. I USUALLY MAKE MY MUM OR DAD READ THE EMAIL AND TELL ME THE CONTENT. THE EMAIL IS USUALLY TOTALLY FINE, BUT I'M ALWAYS GLAD TO HAVE SOMEONE WITH ME IN CASE IT ISN'T.
RECEIVING TOO MANY PHONE CALLS	• AGAIN, PHONE CALLS FROM WORK COLLEAGUES AND BOSSES MAKE ME ANXIOUS. USUALLY IT'S BECAUSE A PHONE CALL MEANS I HAVE TO **DO** SOMETHING, WHICH ADDS STRESS. OR, AS ABOVE, I WONDER IF I'VE DONE SOMETHING WRONG. I ALSO HATE TALKING ON THE PHONE ANYWAY. I HAVE REMOVED VOICEMAIL FROM MY PHONE NOW AND ASK PEOPLE TO EMAIL ME INSTEAD. RECEIVING EMAILS MEAN I DO NOT HAVE TO RESPOND IMMEDIATELY, WHICH IS A LESS STRESSFUL EXPERIENCE.
MY PARTNER BEING TOO TOUCHY-FEELY	• I TELL THEM THAT I DON'T WANT TO DO TOUCHING RIGHT NOW. I HAVE MADE IT CLEAR THAT WHEN I AM STRESSED, THE WORST THING SOMEONE CAN DO IS TRY AND HUG ME. UNFORTUNATELY, MY PARTNER IS THE OPPOSITE AND LIKES BEING HUGGED WHEN HE IS STRESSED. HE NEEDS TO REMEMBER THAT ALTHOUGH IT MAKES HIM FEEL BETTER, IT DOES NOT MAKE ME FEEL BETTER.

My mum and dad tell me that the resolution to the fourth stressor (receiving an email from my boss) is not a good long-term strategy. It works in the short-term but it makes me reliant upon my parents and not to be independent. Imagine if you are in a deep forest and the only way you know how to get out is to follow the path that you have taken before. You use the same route and take that path again and again, because you know it's easy. Going another way might be a bit scary. One day you decide to take a different path. It feels scary but at the end, there's something new. You have a totally different experience and you can go down this path more often. You have expanded your comfort zone, which is good!

The Yerke-Dodson Curve

Unfortunately, like many people with Asperger's Syndrome, I am an extremely hard worker, an extremist, and a perfectionist. This means that when I do something, I work hard at it and I do the very best I can. In my mind, I would either rather do something perfectly or not do it at all - there is no in between.

According to the Yerke-Dodson curve, working too hard for too long causes a decrease in performance and an increase in stress levels. The Yerke-Dodson curve looks like this:

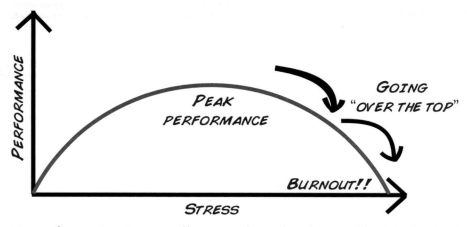

My perfectionism is normally somewhat related to a self-critical voice in my head. Now I think this is because during all my growing up, people have tended to question what I've done and made me feel strange, but I didn't know why. This was especially true for teachers who kept making me feel weird for being quiet, instead of seeing me as a good, hard working pupil. Friends kept questioning why I did not want to join in with their games and I didn't know what to say - these things made me develop thoughts in my head that something must be wrong or that I was doing something wrong and I should try harder.

As I want to be a "good person" this has made me try and try harder, leading me to be a perfectionist. Often this is unrealistic, because I have off days or set my targets too high, and then because of my very strong emotional reactions, it feels catastrophic and devastating. I am trying to see myself like other people. I make mistakes and there are some things I am good at and others I am less good at. But these are the things that make me the person I am.

Pre- and post-mortem anxiety

A really helpful description of the feelings my psychiatrist and I came up with, was that I experience "pre-" and "post-mortem" anxiety episodes.

The pre-mortem concept is descriptive of those feelings of stress, anxiety or worry that I have before the trigger. The post-mortem is descriptive of those feelings that I experience after the trigger.

On the following page is an example of a recent scenario. The trigger is in the middle box:

PRE-MORTEM

SERIOUS STRESS AND ANXIETY ABOUT THE EVENT AND GUILT THAT I PERHAPS SHOULD BE GOING OR FEELINGS THAT I WILL LET PEOPLE DOWN IF I DON'T GO. MY WORK COLLEAGUE DIDN'T SEEM TO TAKE MY "NO" FOR AN ANSWER AND I WAS ASKED NUMEROUS TIMES, LEADING ME TO FEEL SOCIAL PRESSURE. CONSEQUENTLY, I AVOIDED GOING TO WORK FOR THE WHOLE WEEK. I DID NOT WANT TO EXPERIENCE THE SOCIAL PRESSURE.

AN EVENING TALK AFTER WORK

THE BOSS OF MY COMPANY WAS GIVING A TALK TO SOME PEOPLE ON THURSDAY EVENING AFTER WORK. MOST OF MY WORK COLLEAGUES WOULD BE ATTENDING. IT WAS NOT IN MY JOB DESCRIPTION TO ATTEND. THE PREVIOUS WEEK, ONE OF MY COLLEAGUES ASKED ME IF I WAS GOING TO COME AND I SAID "PROBABLY NOT." SHE CONTINUED TO ASK ME UNTIL THE WEDNESDAY BEFORE THE EVENT. THE BOSS HADN'T EXPECTED ME TO GO, SO FOR ME ATTENDANCE WAS OPTIONAL. IT WAS A SOCIAL EVENT AND MY SOCIAL ENERGY TANK IS EMPTY BY EVENING TIME.

POST-MORTEM

EVEN THOUGH I WANTED TO FIND OUT HOW THE EVENING HAD GONE, I WAS TOO UPSET AND WORRIED TO GO IN TO WORK ON FRIDAY TO ASK ABOUT IT. I WAS STRESSED ABOUT THE QUESTIONS THAT MY COLLEAGUE MIGHT ASK ME, AS TO WHY I DIDN'T GO. I WAS STILL UPSET WITH HER FOR THE SOCIAL PRESSURE SHE'D PUT ON ME. CONSEQUENTLY, I AVOIDED GOING TO WORK THE FOLLOWING DAY AND THOUGHT ABOUT HOW IT WAS GOING TO BE WHEN I NEXT WENT IN. THESE FEELINGS CONSUMED THE WEEKEND.

I find these kind of situations really horrible to deal with. My way of coping is avoidance, but this method often makes me feel worse. The longer I avoid having to deal with a situation, the greater the anxiety I feel. If people did not put so much pressure on me to do things and if they were able to understand that when I first said "no" I really did mean no, I would never have to avoid things... or maybe it'd just mean I could avoid things more easily! In this case, I was fully prepared to go in to work on the days preceding the event, but it was the stress of having to face my colleagues that stopped me. But in the end, it was me who suffered because it was me who fell behind on my work and felt unhappy both before and after the event.

I do not think that avoidance is a sensible long-term strategy. Neurotypical people are not going to change. The reason they keep asking me to go out with them is actually because they like my company, so I should take it as a compliment! Intellectually I understand this but, in the moment, it is extremely stressful. Continuous pressure to be asked out and people not taking my "no" for an answer makes me aware that I am quite different from other people, who tend to enjoy these sorts of social events. It is painful to be reminded of these differences sometimes. It is easiest for me to politely decline social invites by email or text message, and I am very clear in letting them know that I am hugely appreciative of being included, even though I do not alway want to accept the invite. I am touched that they ask me.

Social pressure and the build up of stress are probably the biggest causes of my depressive episodes. I can fall into a very low mood for three to four weeks and during this time I will avoid everything. I shut down. I like to describe it as "going into hibernation." I'll stay inside my house, turn my phone off, and ignore all emails except the urgent ones. My mood descends to occasional thoughts of suicide. I'll spend endless hours crying and feeling as though I've fallen into a black hole. But because of how bad I'm feeling I am unable to do the things I enjoy. If I could only do something I enjoyed, there's a chance I'd get out of the hole but, unfortunately I am often completely unable to do anything at all.

Keeping busy is key. My life is made up of "all-encompassing" distractions, which is, essentially, a life in which I am too busy to ruminate.

I think questioning life and your reason for existence are just parts of being human. The difference is, when you have Asperger's Syndrome, you think and question a lot more. It might be quite common for people to 'wish they were dead' when they are feeling low, but when you have Asperger's Syndrome, these thoughts are magnified.

Some episodes of low mood are better than others. The "good" ones do not leave me totally debilitated and the best way I cope is to get out of the house and do something. Often I will sit in a cafe using the computer or just drink tea, not because I want company but just to keep me occupied inside a safe place. Sometimes I'll go and see a movie. The ninety minutes of story sucks me in and for that time I forget about being depressed.

As for the worst moods, they can turn into depressive episodes, and I'll lie in bed endlessly for days, just thinking, usually about nothing in particular. I don't want to do anything I enjoy, my sleep is disturbed and I can't focus. My parents notice my speech slowing down. It is extremely easy for me to fall apart... I just drift into it.

Suicidal depressive episodes

Because Asperger's Syndrome and depression tend to be comorbid, it's understandable that I feel my life could be described as a process like this on the right:

I hate the suicidal episodes and when I recover from these I hope to never feel that way again. Their onset can be very sudden but recovery takes days or even weeks. I become so consumed in my own inner turmoil that even the pleasure of my hobbies disappear.

We all experience emotions, but for people on the autistic spectrum it can be challenging to manage them. When I am sad, I can be extremely sad and forget that sadness is a temporary feeling.

During times of intense sadness, I experience the ultimate feelings that **life has just become too much**. I feel I can no longer cope and do not want to exist in a world that I feel is uninhabitable. I do not have the energy that others seem to have. Even just the simple act of being outside of my house can depress me. Simply "being" on earth and growing up gives me a nagging feeling that there are many things I am unable to do or, simply don't want to - socialising with others, small talk, the "professional/adult" phase of life, living independently. Some of these things are shown overleaf:

ASPERGER'S SYNDROME

FEELING DISCONNECTED, SAD AND ALONE

DEPRESSION

BELIEVING LIFE IS WORTHLESS

SUICIDAL THOUGHTS

The thought of suicide seems like an escape from a world I never wanted to be in from the start.

Thoughts of suicide and dying are not only horrible burdens in my life, they are frightening; I am afraid of the unknown and the devastation I'd cause my family. Thankfully my suicidal thoughts are indeed just thoughts and I know I could never act on them, no matter how much I wanted to. I am very close to my family and my animals.

I do not want to write any more on this subject. It upsets me.

Getting better
Cognitive Behavioural Therapy
When something happens that makes me feel depressed, it can sometimes upset me so much that I'm unable to do the things I usually

enjoy. All the pleasure I get from reading books, lifting weights, cycling and writing stories, just disappears. The effort required to even get started on any of these activities takes too much energy.

A theory I think about a lot is, when we feel low, it's really important to do the things we enjoy and to try and stick to our usual routines. Otherwise, things can spiral out of control. In my mind, this spiral looks like this:

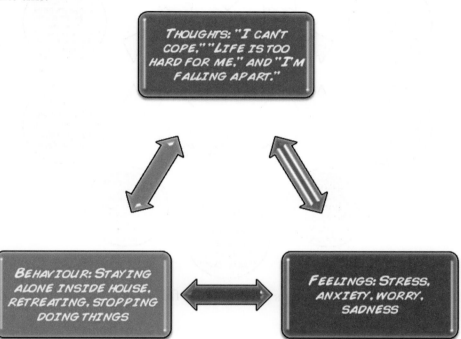

This cycle is actually based on an idea in CBT, which basically states that thoughts, feelings and behaviour are all connected. There will be a trigger in the middle of the cycle. If you look at my cycle you will see that by changing just one of these things will cause the others to change. Depending on your personality, you might find it easier to change either a behaviour, thought or feeling.

The best thing someone can do for me, to get me out of this spiral, is help me take that first step to change my behaviour. This is typically by helping me to do an activity I enjoy. What my mum does is she stops me retreating and gets me doing something I enjoy. This in turn changes my thoughts to "I'm having fun," or "this is wonderful" and feelings become "happy." My mum usually comes up to my room, where I'll be crying in my bed, and she'll suggest coming into the gym to watch me. Another example is my friend, who will give me a pair of his trousers for me to artistically paint, because he knows I like to do this.

I really appreciate the initial push (encouragement) that my mum can give me. After I've finished the first activity I feel better and am more likely to do another activity, without the need for another push. It's really important that someone helps me, because when I am depressed it's as if I can't even be bothered to want to do things that, intellectually, I know will help. Asperger's Syndrome makes emotions a lot more overpowering and exaggerated and sometimes they're so suffocating that all willpower to make positive change just disappears.

Generally, my family know me well enough to distinguish between me not wanting to do something and not being able to do something. For example, my family will know that I don't want to go out with my friend, but they'll know I want to do weightlifting, it's just that I'm too depressed to do it.

Please be aware, if you aren't on the autistic spectrum, that sometimes when an AS says "no" it really does mean no and there's a very fine line between pressurising someone into doing something and providing gentle encouragement. If you love or care about someone with Asperger's Syndrome, it's a good idea to learn how to distinguish and understand these boundaries.

Routine is the most important thing and it is long-term sustainable routines that keep me from feeling depressed. I try and make sure that every day is the same.

Mood states

Sometimes I feel that I only experience a limited range of emotions. Since writing this book, I've actually felt really happy, despite going through some problems in my relationships. Even though these problems have been just as bad as they always were, I have not felt as terrible as I usually do. Writing this book has given me a bit more resilience to just bounce back and keep going!

Everyone has a natural baseline mood state. I think my baseline is lower than the average person's. This means that I am more frequently sad than happy and that when I feel sad, those feelings are more intense than the average person's. I can describe this by considering the three basic human mood states to be sad, normal, and happy.

This is all just my own opinion. There is no concrete way of knowing whether my baseline mood is lower than the average person's. I'm aware that in public people often wear happy faces, even when they feel really horrible inside. It all goes back to the "fakeness" of asking someone how they are and telling them you're well, even if you're not. Sometimes I find the daily interactions of human beings quite "dishonest." Wouldn't the world be better if we all just said how we really feel?

On a scale of 1 to 10, I consider an average person to have a normal mood of 5. When he or she is sad, this might drop to 4. When happy, it might rise to 6.

On the other hand, I think that my normal mood is 4. When I am sad, it plummets straight to 2 and misses out 3, because I experience more intense feelings of sadness than the average person. When happy, my mood might rise to 5. Notice that my normal mood is always a bit lower than someone else's normal mood (mine is 4 and theirs is 5). My sad mood is more intense than someone else's (mine is 2 whereas their own is 4). My happy mood is the same as the average person's baseline mood (both 5).

Writing this is a bit upsetting. It makes me wonder whether anyone really understands anyone at all. If people always tell me they're OK, even when they're not, how can I even attempt to help them feel better? How can we call each other friends? My natural inclination is to always be honest and sincere. I wish others would be.

The following graph illustrates perception of my own feelings well:

MOOD STATES

I have often said that I never really feel happy, or at least, I don't experience happiness in the same way that others seem to. My happy seems to be like everyone else's normal.

I don't know if there's any truth to what I'm saying, but it does make some sense to me. It's known that people with Asperger's Syndrome tend to be overly sensitive and have strong emotions, so maybe there's some truth here.

It has taken... 24 years(:)), but I think that finally I am accepting of having a low natural mood state. It just means I have to manage it appropriately and recognise the differences between myself and someone else. Of course this is easy to say when I am feeling happy (as I am now). As we all well know, during low periods, everything can become hopeless.

Emotion
Most of the time I feel very flat or neutral, interspersed with long periods of depression, anxiety and short bursts of happiness. I do not feel that I have ever experienced euphoria or joy, in the way that others do. I am happy sometimes. I look forward to things but I don't believe what

I experience are feelings of excitement. Instead, I think I experience stronger feelings of anxiety and anticipation.

> I would describe happiness as being a calmer version of joy or euphoria. All 3 are in the same emotional "group" but I don't think happiness is as powerful as the other two.

I experience very strong negative emotions, such as anxiety, isolation, and sadness. I consider even my positive emotions as only weakly positive. I feel that the intensity of these negative emotions is far, **far** stronger than the intensity of positive ones. When I was a teenager and into my early twenties I only ever really felt depressed. When I experience happiness, it usually only lasts for a few minutes. Most of the time I am in a baseline mood state. Often I feel guilty when I think I have upset someone or have not done something I should have. I feel anger and frustration... which I can only just control.

I have to be careful about things I see on the television or in films. I am easily upset by scenes that may not have any effect on someone else.

Connections to songs

I tend to only like one or two songs at any one time period. For this time period (days or weeks) I will only listen to those songs and nothing else. When I was at college I listened to X and Y and now every time I hear those songs all I think about is very specific moments in college. Unfortunately this also means that songs that I loved but listened to during bad times (e.g. school or bad relationships), I can no longer listen to any more - because they upset me greatly.

For example, for the first two weeks at the start of secondary school I loved the song A by artist B. I enjoyed listening to it so much and played it on repeat for two weeks. I did not listen to anything else during this time.

> It's a bit Aspie to do repeating tasks, such as repeat a song over and over again. But NTs repeat songs, too!

Now, every single time I hear song A by artist B I no longer enjoy it. I like the song but not the memory it reminds me of. It makes me feel as unhappy as I did during the first two weeks at school. Suddenly I feel eleven years old again - lonely, different, left out, rejected, miserable.

It is horrible if I am in a public place and I hear a song which takes me back to unpleasant memories. My dad says that he only links songs and events generally, but for me the link is incredibly specific and the memory is very intense.

I am often overly emotional. It can appear strange to others that I might burst into tears because I woke up an hour later than usual. I have very volatile and powerful mood swings and can go from feeling happy to feeling devastated in a matter of minutes.

A child or young person with Asperger's Syndrome will often only have a limited vocabulary to describe their emotions. They may also find it hard to vary their expressions in response to how they are feeling. An NT should learn to ask the right questions as the AS will then be able to adequately explain their feelings. People with AS often have trouble recognising and describing their feelings and isues. Stressful situations are problematic.

I find it hard to feel the more intermediate emotions. I recognise feelings of sadness or anxiety because they are so powerful and occur all the time. I am less able to recognise the "in between" feelings such as uncertainty, agitation, irritability, and impatience. These feelings always tend to lead to the more powerful ones, such as sadness. Consequently, I find it hard to describe my feelings to others. My mum says I always use the word "sad" to describe my feelings but when we actually talk about this, it often appears that what I'm actually experiencing is stress or frustration, etc. Unfortunately whatever negative things I feel, they always lead to sadness being the main emotion.

Finding a purpose in life

I'll be honest, before I wrote this book I was going through a depression. One of the reasons I was depressed was because I felt I had no purpose. I am convinced now, having written this, that there probably is no purpose in life, other than enjoying the journey and other people - but this is stressful for me... so I have to build my own purpose and find my own meaning. If you have Asperger's Syndrome you've probably felt at least as confused as me your entire life. That misplaced, "alien" feeling is internally and eternally with us.

I do not believe that Asperger's Syndrome alone is the cause of depression, but I believe that Asperger's Syndrome exaggerates feelings of depression. I feel lost and left out in social situations and uncomfortable meeting new people. Other people may also experience similar feelings, yet I wonder whether mine are more intense than theirs. It pains me that I am not excited nor fulfilled by the "normal" things, such as love, a family or career, that others seemingly live for. I think life would be easier if I had life goals such as these, for they are probably much easier to achieve than trying to make sense of a world that seems like it is the wrong planet.

10.
The Now and Beyond

What I'm up to now

Work

From a young age I always wanted to be a writer. I write in the hope that one day I will publish something and that it will be the 'making of me.' I haven't sold my books yet, so in the meantime I am working as an internet marketeer. My work is not intellectually challenging and I find it boring most of the time, but I work alone, from home, to my own schedule, so it suits me and the people I work with are lovely.

For the last couple of years my dad and I have been working hard at mastering the financial markets (Forex trading or Foreign Exchange). I enjoy it, because looking for trends in charts is exciting and educational; and to be successful at trading a "different" way of thinking and seeing is needed. I hope that soon I'll have a full time income from trading. It is a solitary "job" that requires as much time and risk as I choose. I am in control and I like that. It would be a dream for me to wake up, spend 1 hour entering some trades, spent the rest of my day doing weightlifting and writing, and spend 1 hour checking the trades in the evening. It would give me so much freedom. Maybe everyone would like that!

In addition, I love trading because it has strengthened the bond between my daddy and I. We have lots in common and our trading is always something we can talk about. We are a partnership and our trading is a "secret club."

Education

I have been to University and completed my undergraduate and masters degrees. Currently, my intention is to do a PhD on the prevention of valgus collapse (when the knees track inward toward each other) in the squat exercise, particularly in weightlifting. I am obsessively interested in the valgus collapse and would like to further my education to keep my brain really active. I do not know where my PhD would lead or whether I would go on to have a career in this field. I can imagine being very good at studying to this higher level, because I am dedicated, motivated and have always been a self-learner. I am worried about becoming a student again, I feel "out of touch" with the social and committed nature of education. However, I believe that if I survived before then I can survive again!

Since writing this book, my interest in starting the PhD has lessened...
I now fully recognise just how much I love writing. It's my number one
passion, second only to weightlifting, and I really wish I could make a
living from it.

Home

I am still living at home with my parents and my sister. Today, she is
moving away to Kent for five weeks and I will miss her. She is a part of
my routine and I am still learning to make new routines for the times
she isn't here. I live a very simple but fulfilling life. Every day is the same.
It involves doing paper rounds, weightlifting, working and writing. I do
not get bored.

Relationships

I am single and happy. I do not want to be in a relationship right now.
Romantic relationships are very complicated. When I am part of one, I
use up a lot of energy working out emotions and thoughts - or feeling
stressed - when I suppose other people just enjoy the feelings and are
more relaxed. I am really busy with my life right now, writing my books
and doing weightlifting. I don't have enough energy to expend on anything else! I need to be alone a lot, so that I can refill my social energy
tank.

There are lots of times I feel truly unaware or oblivious to both my
gender and my sexuality. It is very difficult for me to have a romantic
relationship. At any time I can have a shutdown. There are times when
I have to be alone for several days. I do not like hugging. A friendly
handshake or a kiss on the cheek could ruin my entire day if I'm not in
the mood.

I have two female friends, both older than me. One of them is a writer.
The other makes fancy dress and costumes for pantomines and theatre
performances.

Future

I wonder whether I could be successful at being a writer about
Asperger's Syndrome and raising awareness of the condition. By

"successful," I am really referring to achieving that state of happiness that other people seem to achieve so much more easily than me.

I have faith that if I could do well in educating others by writing about Asperger's Syndrome, then maybe I could feel happy and "right" living on this wrong planet!

How my Asperger's has changed as I've become older

I wanted to end my book on a positive note. I really hope you found it interesting or even uplifting.

From a young age, I always knew I was different from other children; and since I was diagnosed with Asperger's Syndrome I've realised that my anxieties and low mood are just part of it, which has made them somewhat "easier" to cope with. I honestly can't say exactly how I felt different, I just did. Deep inside it was an innate, isolating feeling. Since I was far too shy to ever talk to anyone about who I really was and what I liked doing (writing stories, playing reality simulation games addictively), I always felt lonely. Looking back, I wonder whether the reason I loved writing stories, creating characters and lives in my video games, was because they were all avenues of "escaping" from myself. I could completely become someone else and live my life through them. Put simply, **I could be happy**.

In some ways I feel my Asperger's Syndrome gets more obvious as I get older, but maybe that's because I was only diagnosed a year ago. It's hard to really work out how it's changed, having been undiagnosed for 23 years. I also don't remember much of my early childhood - I think my parents seemed to deal with all my problems for me. Probably the hardest thing about Asperger's Syndrome as an adult is that the comorbid conditions can creep in. Depression can come on because of the lack of friendships. Social anxiety begins due to the decreased time I spend with people and having less routine than in my school days.

My "self-awareness" increases every day. Some days I am better at coping with the challenges of life, but other days I feel life is a lot more difficult. Every day is a new one.

In some ways I feel I am more sensitive now, or maybe I'm just more aware of my senses? I'm extremely aware of sounds and light when I am in bed at night and I wear earplugs and an eye mask to help me sleep. I don't remember needing these as a child, though my bedroom did always have blackout blinds. I still don't like being touched and people who know me well know not to touch me, not without a warning first.

I love how I am a lot more confident in my abilities, for example I know and realise I am very good at weightlifting but less good at public speaking (and it's something I'll probably never want to do). Life has been hard but gradually I care less what people think of me and feel more comfortable being "myself" in public. There are many days where I no longer have to wear my normal mask at all!

Nowadays I'll wear the same clothes every day or I'll leave the house without brushing my hair. I'll wear torn trousers quite happily (it just happens that sometimes my trouser leg gets caught in my bike chain etc. I am a cyclist, it's what happens! Why should I have to buy new trousers every time this happens when it's already a challenge just to find one pair that I like?) Generally, I always try and speak my mind. Of course there are lots of times when I feel self-conscious and shy but mostly, I try to focus on observing and understanding the neurotypical world, rather than what the world thinks of me.

I can honestly say that having Asperger's will no doubt always be very challenging, but growing older is the best kept secret. I am a lot happier, more comfortable and more self aware than I was when I was younger. Many women with Asperger's Syndrome are not diagnosed until their late twenties, or even their forties and fifties, such as Wendy Lawson. The diagnosis often comes as a relief - it gives us a "home." I have spoken to a lot of people older than me (both spectrum and non-spectrum), who all say that **as you grow up you care less about what others think of you**. Life becomes a lot more liberating.

A disability puts you at a disadvantage, before you've even attempted what you want to attempt! e.g. You want to learn tennis. The NT will go to class, follow instructions and make friends. The AS will have to overcome social anxiety before starting the class, might need written instructions rather than verbal, and may not immediately make friends or have someone to pair up with. Most things (school, clubs, activities, events etc.) were made for NTs by NTs. We are the minority in an NT world - everything is harder!

I used to wish that socialising could be as easy for me as it was for other people. But not anymore! What I lack in social skills, I more than make up for in my attention to detail, diligence, creativity, unique perspective of life and relentless intellectual curiosity. Also, I have exceptional focus and dedication to my hobbies and interests. I would not change my personality for anything.

If you are young and you regularly hear people telling you that "school/ university days are the best years of your life" please do not feel you have to believe them! That used to make me feel incredibly, incredibly depressed. Those years were my worst ones. It does get better. I am happy now.

Writing this book has been a self-discovery and enlightening process. I have realised that I cannot resent the world because I feel that my life should be easier than it is. I do not think that anyone should ever assume that the world will just fit in with them without any effort on their own part. Both NT and AS people are free spirits... and we are all owed compassion and equality. However, it is up to the individual to have an open mind, tolerance, flexibility and a willingness to want to work with others, not against them. It is up to us to work to the best of our ability. We have a choice whether to make life easier or harder than it it is now. You can choose to be happy or sad with an autism spectrum disorder. Believe me, it's a lot nicer being happy.

Believe in yourself - because you CAN live a relatively 'normal' life

Particularly when you are young, it is very easy to lose faith in not only the world, but also **who you are**. The teenage years are very fragile. You want to fit in but for some reason, you just can't...

Like you, I have asked myself those questions, such as why my life is so different to other people's? And why do I feel so "alien?"

Please have hope and faith. I can assure you that things CAN and they DO change - you just have to be willing, flexible, and hard working. Most of all, you have to believe in yourself.

Between the ages of 11-16, I was incredibly unhappy (clinically depressed), and because I was so shy and suffered from mutism, I was unable to explain to anyone how I was feeling. Even if I could, I did not have the words. I would not have known WHAT to say. I just knew that I was different...

I was really happy at home, when I was doing my hobbies. Outside of the house, it was devastating. Life was very hard and very cruel for a long time. I had the same questions that you have. "Why am I like this?" "Just why is life so hard for me, when it seems so easy for other people?" "Why do I have everything, a good home, money, family, academic capability, yet feel inside that I have nothing and that my life is meaningless?"

But I worked hard. Here I am today, 25 years old. I have been to a mainstream neurotypical school. I have done my A levels. I have been to university. I have achieved a first class undergraduate degree and a masters.

I run a successful business now. I choose my own hours. I fit my work around my weightlifting, not the other way round.

I have loved. I have been loved. **I AM loved**.

I have friends. I have two wonderful friends for the first time in what has been many years.

I have found the most amazing hobby (weightlifting) that I fully immerse myself into and it makes me unbelievably happy...

For the first time in many years, I can see the future. And it is a good sight.

On a final note...

I just want you to know, particularly if you are young and miserable with Asperger's Syndrome, that life WILL change. With the right support in place, you can and WILL live a comfortable and relatively 'normal' life.

I cannot change the world, but I hope this book might change the world, even just for one person. **If I can do it, you can too.**

If you're not on the autistic spectrum, please do not make these sorts of comments to someone who is on the spectrum:

If someone's opened up to you to tell you they've got AS, please appreciate it. Many of us are very careful about who we tell about it and, especially for me, it takes a lot of "courage" to tell someone.

Some of the responses above make me feel quite angry and upset. Like most of us on the spectrum, every day when we get up and go out into our non autistic world (the "wrong planet"), we've learned to adjust and put on our normal masks; it takes a huge amount of effort and energy. If everyone did feel this way, for example if everyone had sensory overload problems, then there would be a lot more support available.

> BUT A LOT OF THOSE PROBLEMS YOU TALK ABOUT, I HAVE THEM TOO. THEY'RE QUITE NORMAL. I HAVE THAT PROBLEM TOO!

I'm "upset" because it feels that some people think they know me well enough to tell me I don't have Asperger's and it's incredibly frustrating to receive remarks from people who don't really know about my condition and what it really means; it's often shrugged off or disregarded and I feel belittled or unheard. I love this quote:

'The difference between high functioning autism and low functioning autism is that high functioning means your deficits are ignored, and low functioning means your assets are ignored.' (Laura Tisoncik[1], n.d.)

Although on the surface it may seem I cope really well, I do have difficulties and need support in various areas of my life. Although I value the term 'high functioning', it can sometimes make my condition seem less debilitating than it really is.

I can tell you that, unless you are a sufferer, or unless you've dedicated significant time to finding out all you can about AS, then you can never truly know what we experience. Most people don't really have any idea. I know they're only trying to help but the remarks above, that are often passed, are probably some of the most unhelpful things you can say to me. Most people with Asperger's Syndrome have developed such convincing "facades" that people just don't see the struggles we have when we're on our own - they are totally unaware of the depression, the black holes, the loneliness we may experience every day.

I have struggled. Life has been hard. It's only as I have grown up I realise that you have the choice to be either happy or sad in life - whether you are AS or NT.

I am really lucky that my loved ones take a big interest in AS and spend a lot of time learning about it.

If you really want to help your AS loved one, the best thing you can do is learn about AS and read all you can about it.

Good luck on your journey together.

---

1 Tisoncik, L. (n.d.). Autism Favourite Quotes. Available: http://www.circleofmoms.com/autismaspergerspdd-awareness/favorite-autism-quotes-569012. Last accessed 19th Sep 2013.

Appendix 1

Comparisons of school and university:

School	My experience	University	My experience
You had to attend school every day Monday to Friday, from around 9am to 3pm	This was horrific for me. There was just too much social overload. It was really draining	Classes were very flexible. Some days I didn't have to go in to university at all. Some days finished early, some started late etc.	Much better. The time spent out of class was used to recover. The days I didn't have to go in were used as 'resting days'
Not very many social events outside of school	Good. I mostly managed to keep my socialising inside school and keep my evenings and weekends free	Huge emphasis on social life and going out in the evenings to clubs etc.	Very hard. I often felt left out. I missed out on a big part of university life, and even though I didn't want to do the socialising it left me feeling lonely
Lots of bullying	Because school was so small (comparatively), everyone knew everything about each other. I was bullied a lot	Everyone had grown up a bit and bullying didn't happen	I enjoyed life without being bullied

School	My experience	University	My experience
The teachers really helped you manage your workload. You had a diary etc.	It was easy to stay organised and not miss deadlines	Big lack of workload management. You are expected to cope all on your own and meet deadlines and attend sporadic lab classes etc.	I really liked this aspect of university because I was able to work at my own pace. I am an organised person so having so little help suited me fine
Busy corridors, noisy, bright lighting	Traumatic. I hate crowds, loud noises and bright lights	The same. Busy corridors, noisy, bright lighting	Traumatic. I hate crowds, loud noises and bright lights. At least I was able to find quieter routes in to the building at non-peak times
Busy, hectic canteen and restrictions on going home at lunch times	For the whole of school I missed eating lunch because I was so afraid of the crazy canteen	Busy canteen but due to the flexible class structure I was able to go home at lunch times	Going home was really helpful because it meant I could always eat my own food in the peace and quiet of my own home. It gave me time to reconstruct myself

School	My experience	University	My experience
School uniform	I hated wearing uncomfortable formal clothes	You could wear whatever you wanted	Brilliant. I could wear sportswear or baggy clothes without having to tuck my shirt in. There was a good sense of individuality at university. I even customised my lab coat with an artistically painted design
Compulsory lessons	Lessons such as Drama were horrendous. I used to dread them and stay up wide awake the night before. I was nervous about acting or talking in front of the class, it was really scary	Chemistry was my subject	It was not forced upon me to take any classes I didn't want to. Extra activities, such as joining the university acting or sports societies were entirely optional

School	My experience	University	My experience
Group work	I hated group work. It's very insensitive how all the teachers just assumed it was okay for me to participate in groups. Taking part in group work is one of the most stressful things for me. It is never something I want to do. Often you were just put with a random person or group	Sharing lab work with someone else	Manageable. I had the same partner for the whole of university, who became my friend

School	My experience	University	My experience
Strong relationship with teachers	Because we were just children, the teachers did look after you and there was a sense of knowing one another/ bonding	Didn't really know my lecturers	My impression was that lecturers were really researchers who sometimes gave lectures. They really just gave you the information, and everything else was up to you. But it was okay, I liked the independence and maturity required to handle this

Stay in touch with the girl with the curly hair

Facebook:
www.facebook.com/thegirlwiththecurlyhair

Twitter:
www.twitter.com/alisthelioness
www.twitter.com/curlyhairedgirl

Email:
alis@thegirlwiththecurlyhair.co.uk

Website:
www.thegirlwiththecurlyhair.co.uk

If you enjoyed this book, please consider writing an Amazon review.

Why do I get up in the morning? I get up in the morning to write this book... and when it's finished, I'll write another one. I believe I can find peace and sense of the world, by writing and reading about other people's experiences of the condition that is

ASPERGER'S SYNDROME.

"I have low functioning AS and I am concerned that my son to be might be born with it too. You help me put my feelings into words and scenarios which help me make sense of these things so that when my son arrives we can understand each other really well. Even though I have AS I have trouble understanding it myself sometimes and I don't realise how some of the things I think and feel are really caused from having AS."
Hayleigh, Australia

"Your insights give me a good feeling. My 3 year old daughter is ASD, and isn't able to express her thoughts as an adult can, so I take your words and try to remember them as I imagine they apply to her as well. Thank you for your part in helping a mom through this journey!"
Heather, USA

"I love so much your page, because the girl with the curly hair shows how we feel everyday! And it is an huge support to feel less alone for me. You have to keep going on, because you give to me (and all) hope."
Juliette, France

"If you or someone you know have or think you might have Asperger's Syndrome, you need to see the great stuff the girl with the curly hair is doing. I've never seen such well presented and easy to understand information on AS."
Stewart, UK

"You are one of the first who's had the knack at explaining ME in words so that others can understand.

It's just this huge relief to see somebody else 'gets it.'"
Anonymous, USA

"It is a delight to see how much you've put into the curly hair project, both on this page and on your website. I've barely even scratched the surface of it as well, there's so much of it!!

The passion and dedication you're putting into this is truly admirable, not just for women but for both genders, as a lot of what you've posted applies to both."
James, UK

"Thank you for spreading messages and useful information about Asperger's to the world. You make a great ambassador for all the Aspie communities. And many posts clearly describe the inside out life of an Aspie."
Anonymous, Malaysia

"Thank you for teaching me to be a better mum to my kids. Your work has taught me so much and I've also shared your charts with their teachers and it has helped them immensely! You are amazing!!!"
Desiree, USA

"I think about you and your Facebook page often since my AS girlfriend introduced me to it. It's a great page and very very interesting and helpful!! I have learned a lot."
Michael, UK

"My 13 year old daughter said Alis is the first person with Asperger's Syndrome who she understands!"
Nicola, UK

"This is proof- there's others out there like me, I'm not the only one. Thank you so much the girl with the curly hair."
Erik, Netherlands